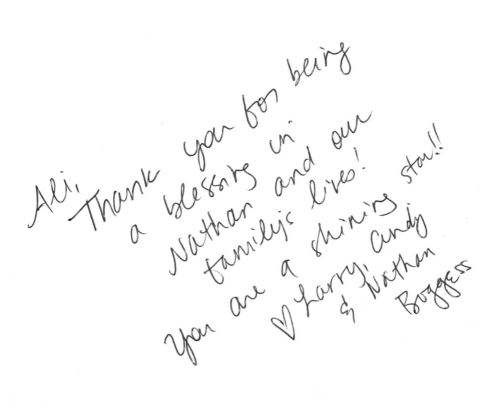

Ali,
Thank you for being a blessing in Nathan and our families lives! You are a shining star!!

♡ Larry, Cindy & Nathan Boggess

What people are saying about …

becoming myself

"Stasi Eldredge and I have a lot in common. For years I was paralyzed by fear and insecurity—trapped in my own prison. God led me on a journey of freedom that is enabling me to become who He created me to be. If you need true transformation from the inside out, I encourage you to read *Becoming Myself.* Learn to see yourself as God sees you!"

Betty Robison, author of *Free to Be Me* and cohost of the "LIFE Today" television program

"Every daughter wants to make her father proud, and there is no greater way for you to glorify our heavenly Father than by becoming who God created you to be. *Becoming Myself* is a masterfully woven tapestry of Scripture, vulnerability, and practical applications as Stasi invites you to be you!"

Lisa Bevere, speaker and author of *Girls with Swords* and *Lioness Arising*, Messenger International

"Reading Stasi Eldredge's *Becoming Myself* is like spending time with a close friend who understands firsthand the inner battles women face and who wants more than anything to help us win those battles. The buildup of internalized negative messages planted deep into a woman's soul through emotional and sexual abuse and life's losses and disappointments produces paralyzing self-doubt and fear. Stasi offers hope that confronting these battles can be the making of us and may actually be how God equips us for the kingdom work He calls us to do."

Carolyn Custis James, author of *Half the Church*

"*Becoming Myself* is a lavish book. Stasi is generous with her wisdom, her humor, and her story, and the impact is a deeper thirst to live with that kind of lavish freedom. Stasi mines the Scriptures and her own life to bring a weighty and enjoyable book—one that calls us deeper, deeper into being ourselves because it pleases God's heart. Reading this book is like sitting with Stasi as she tells the tales of all that has shaped and transformed her life. There's a boatload of hope in this book—hope that I *can* be truly myself as Jesus sheds His love for me abroad in me. Get this book. It is a treasure."

Jan Meyers Proett, counselor, speaker, and author
of *The Allure of Hope* and *Listening to Love*

"It seems that everywhere I've spoken over the past decade, a handful of people mistake me for Stasi Eldredge (because our first and last names are so similar). It's become quite comical. Then when I saw her book title, *Becoming Myself,* I couldn't help but laugh at the irony of it—a book about 'becoming myself,' written by the person I'm most often mistaken for! But the irony didn't stop there. As I pored over these pages, I realized that Stasi and I really *could* be the same person—and my suspicion is that you're going to say the same thing when you read this book! We all have the same voices of shame echoing in our brains, the same drive to strictly discipline ourselves, the same notion that someday we'll succeed in doing better and get our act totally together. It's so exhausting and self-defeating! But get ready to finally get comfortable in the skin God put you in, as Stasi reveals exactly how to get off that crazy train! *Becoming Myself* is a stunningly beautiful reminder that we're deeply loved, accepted, and celebrated by God—not *someday,* but *right now!*"

Shannon Ethridge, MA, bestselling author of twenty
books, including the Every Woman's Battle series

"The thing about Stasi Eldredge's writing is not just that she is wise or real or experienced—but that she imbues all those truths with her warmth so she feels like a friend urging us to step into our beautiful, image-bearing selves.

Simultaneously she urges us to step up and step out of every crippling, counterfeit thing that keeps us from the only thing, the everything, that is Christ."

Ashley Cleveland, songwriter, musician,
and author of *Little Black Sheep*

"Who am I becoming? Who do I want to become? Is there an honest woman out there who can help me on my journey? I answer YES! Stasi Eldredge has written her *becoming* story, and I applaud Stasi for being honest, vulnerable, and just down-to-earth *real* in *Becoming Myself.* How refreshing for a Christian leader to pour hope into God's women by being real! Let Stasi take you by the hand and gently lead you to God's dream of you. Read this book! It is transformational!"

Linda Dillow, author of *Calm My Anxious Heart*
and *What's It Like to Be Married to Me?*

"*Becoming Myself* reads like a love letter to ourselves, written with the hand of Jesus gently curled around ours as we hold the pen. His guiding hand puts a whole new slant on the interpretation of both the pain and the glory buried deep within our stories. If you've ever suffered under the Goldilocks syndrome of feeling 'too this' or 'not enough that,' Stasi Eldredge will guide you along the path to 'just right' in Christ."

Kimberly L. Smith, author of *Passport through Darkness* and copresident of Make Way Partners

stasi eldredge

becoming *myself*

embracing God's
dream of you

David C Cook®
transforming lives together

BECOMING MYSELF
Published by David C Cook
4050 Lee Vance View
Colorado Springs, CO 80918 U.S.A.

David C Cook Distribution Canada
55 Woodslee Avenue, Paris, Ontario, Canada N3L 3E5

David C Cook U.K., Kingsway Communications
Eastbourne, East Sussex BN23 6NT, England

The graphic circle C logo is a registered trademark of David C Cook.

Some names have been changed throughout to protect privacy.

The website addresses recommended throughout this book are offered as a
resource to you. These websites are not intended in any way to be or imply an
endorsement on the part of David C Cook, nor do we vouch for their content.

LCCN 2013936044
Hardcover ISBN 978-1-4347-0535-8
International Trade Paperback Edition ISBN 978-0-7814-0995-7
eISBN 978-1-4347-0597-6

The Team: Terry Behimer, Karen Lee-Thorp, Nick Lee, Caitlyn Carlson, Karen Athen
Cover Design: Amy Konyndyk

Printed in the United States of America
First Edition 2013

1 2 3 4 5 6 7 8 9 10

051713

For John
You, I love.

contents

1

does anyone ever
really change?

My husband's parents were coming for a visit—reason enough to paint the basement, let alone clean the refrigerator, as any woman knows. When company comes, we put our best foot forward, especially when the company coming is the in-laws. We color our hair, buy a new top, hide the nail holes in the wall with toothpaste; we make one more pass at teaching the dog to sit and our children to read, sit up straight, and chew with their mouths closed—all within a period of about forty-eight hours.

A few days before their arrival, John's mother mentioned that she wanted to take me to get a massage during their stay.

Yikes.

I had never had a massage before, and the thought of some stranger touching my body was *not* an appealing one to me. My mother-in-law assured me I would love it. I hoped I would. But I didn't think so. You see, I didn't love my body. Far to the contrary—I was embarrassed by it. I didn't

exactly relish the thought of exposing it to the hands of some strange mas-
seuse. How does one lose ten pounds in four days? I googled it. It involves
lemon juice and cayenne pepper. I couldn't do it. But I had to go. It was
her gift to me. She was excited to give it. I needed to be grateful to receive
it. Or at least appear to be.

After checking in at the spa, we were both given soft, luxurious bathrobes and a pair of plastic slippers. We were shown to the changing area
with lockers for our clothes, purses, and jewelry. I looked at Mom and
asked with dread, "*All* our clothes?"

"Yes, all your clothes." Seeing the look on my face, she graciously
added, "You can keep your underwear on if you'd be more comfortable."

Ummmm … *Yes.*

The time came for me to try to discreetly undress and put on the
bathrobe while not exposing an inch of skin to any woman who might
happen to glance my way. That was difficult, but I was determined. I was
also uncomfortable. Then I was mortified. The one-size-fits-all bathrobe
didn't fit *all*. I was too large for it.

Securing my nonemotional, matter-of-fact face, I put my clothes back
on and headed out front to speak the dreaded words, "This doesn't fit me.
Do you have anything larger?"

They did have a larger robe. They had a man's robe. An extra large
man's robe. In a much different color from the women's robes.

Here we were at this spa, sitting in the waiting room, surrounded by
lots of other women wearing matching bathrobes, and I was wearing one
that might as well have been flashing an orange neon glow-in-the-dark sign
that read "obese."

I went into the bathroom and cried. I vowed never to be in that situation again.

But eleven years later, one hundred pounds down and ninety back up, I
was. Different gift. Different spa. Different robe. But no larger size available.

Why don't I have victory here? Why haven't I been able to maintain lasting change? What is wrong with me? Have you ever felt that? Maybe not with your weight, but with some area of your life?

why here and not there?

I remember well the laughter of an older friend over my inability to lose weight. It wasn't cruel laughter; it was lighthearted. With delight in her eyes and a deep sense of knowing, she asked me, how hard did I think it would be for God to take care of that struggle for me? With a snap of her fingers she demonstrated how quickly he could remove all compulsion to use food to comfort myself, numb my pain, or simply escape.

Well, then, if it would be so easy for him, why wasn't he doing it? I certainly had asked him, pleaded with him, cried out to him for help here. So it's *his* fault, really. That's how I felt.

The thing is, I *have* experienced change—miraculous change. Shortly before becoming a Christian in my early twenties, I had wanted to clean up my act. I'd become acutely aware of my dependence on drugs and alcohol, how I was using them every single day in order to endure my life or at least keep the pain at bay. I decided that I would quit cold turkey. I wouldn't smoke pot, do any drugs, or drink alcohol, and while I was at it, I'd stop eating sugar, too. I didn't make it twenty-four hours. On any front.

Dang.

One night, in desperation and hope, I gave up trying to fix my life and collapsed into the waiting arms of Jesus, responding to his invitation, "Come to me, all you who are weary and burdened, and I will give you rest. Take my yoke upon you and learn from me.… For my yoke is easy and my burden is light" (Matt. 11:28–30). I had finished reading the verses and fallen on the floor.

I was weary beyond words. My life was a shambles. My heart was shattered, and I had done much of the shattering myself. I confessed my deep need to God and asked him to come for me, if he would have me. I gave my life to Jesus, mess that it was, mess that I was, and he *did* come for me. My little salvation prayer worked.

Two weeks later, I realized that I had not smoked any pot, taken any drugs, or drunk any alcohol since my prayer. Two weeks. This broke all records from the previous ten years. This was a true blue, bona fide miracle. God delivered me from even the *desire* to use anything. I didn't want to, and I didn't need to. I was awakened to my soul and to the presence of God and to hope. And yeah, baby, there were hard days in that season, but the myriad of stories I have of God's miraculous coming for me in the nick of time are glorious.

Back then, food wasn't a huge issue. I wasn't overweight, and I wasn't inclined to binge. That came later. But when it came, it came with an unyielding power that all my prayer and efforts, repentance, determination, and willpower could not budge.

God delivered me once. Why wouldn't he snap his fingers and do it again?

Many women feel like a failure as a woman. I know that oftentimes I do. A failure as a human being, really. It has affected just about everything I have done and everything I have been kept from doing. But I am not a failure as a human being or as a woman. In some core place deep within, I know this. I fail, yes. But *I* am not a failure. I disappoint. But *I* am not a disappointment. Yet when I find myself again in this place—losing the battle for my beauty, my body, my heart—I can sure feel like a failure in every way. And isn't that true for every woman? Don't we all have secret places where we are not living in the victory we long for, places that color how we see ourselves? Doesn't it go on to become a barrier between us and the people in our lives? A wall separating us from the love of God?

Or is it just me?

I didn't think so.

Sometimes we feel hopeless to ever change simply because our personal history is filled with our failed attempts to change. Where was that angel who was supposed to be guarding our tongue and preventing those harsh words from lashing out at our children? What happened to that fruit of the Spirit that was empowering us to be self-controlled and pass by the donut section? God has not given me a spirit of fear, so why am I so consumed with worry over my children, my finances, my future? If the fear of man is a snare, why do I still find I am terrified of exposing my true self and then being rejected? My bondage to food has been revealed as a liar and a thief, and yet in the moment of pain, too often I still turn to it.

God knows.

God knows.

He has not turned his face away. The very fact that we long for the change we do is a sign that *we are meant to have it*. Our very dissatisfaction with our weaknesses and struggles points to the reality that continuing to live in them is not our destiny.

Read those two sentences again. Let hope rise. Why are you struggling with the things you do? There is a reason. It is found in the life you have lived, the wounds you have received, what you have come to believe about yourself because of them, and not having a clue how to bear your sorrow. It is also because of who you are meant to be.

It is not too late. It is not too hard. You are not too much. God's mercies are new every morning. There is mercy in his eyes even now.

rising to the occasion

I hate spiders. They are creepy. Movies have been made about giant poisonous spiders invading from the Amazon. There's an old movie about a massive spider hiding in train tunnels, and then of course there's that nasty giant spider who chased down a poor helpless hobbit. Spiders. Yuck. They are guaranteed to draw screams.

I used to scream when I came upon one in the bathroom. I was almost twelve years old when my mother refused to come and kill the hairy terrifying thing in the sink for me. "Don't be ridiculous. You do it." I mustered all my bravery into a wad of toilet paper and squished the poor thing. Afterward, I was pretty sure that all of this spider's relatives, all of its aunts and uncles and brothers and sisters and mother and father, were going to come after me for revenge. They would probably creep up on me sometime during the night. Yes, it was an irrational fear. Well, maybe. Anyway, I hate spiders.

When I was twenty-three I lived for a year by myself in a one-room cottage behind a friend's home. It was tiny. It was perfect for me. It had one drawback. You guessed it—it was filled with spiders. I would wake each morning to at least ten spread out on the walls, greeting me to the new day. When I returned from work at night, a dozen more would be staggered around the room to welcome me home. I adjusted. I no longer scream when I see a spider (usually), and yes, I can kill them all by myself. If I have to.

My living situation, growing up and out, forced me to take responsibility for my little world. You know the saying: "Adapt or die." Or maybe it was, "That which does not kill you makes you stronger." Either way, I needed to support myself. Pay rent. Buy car insurance. Plan a wedding. Kill or ignore invading spiders. I needed to rise to the occasion of my life. It took practice. Killing that first spider as a young woman on the verge of adolescence was a milestone for me, and over time I became a woman who possesses the capacity not to be paralyzed in the presence of an eight-legged creature. I changed. And that's a good thing.

Maybe you never were afraid of spiders. Maybe you are like my friend Sam, who captures any and all invading insects—yes, even spiders—gently transporting them to her backyard and releasing them to buggy freedom. But you do have those places in your life where you want to grow up. You want to be free.

I believe you can.

I believe God is in the business of setting us free, making each of us into the woman he always wanted us to be. The woman *we* always wanted to be. Sometimes he does it with the flip of a switch. But not most of the time (as you well know). Most of the time God invites us into a *process* of change—a process where by his grace we can rise to the occasion of our lives. But before we talk about that process, there are a few things we need to get straight.

shame and discipline won't cut it

First, shame is not an agent of change.

Like a shot of caffeine in the morning, self-loathing may propel us onto the road of change, but we will find that hatred of self only leads us onto a never-ending roundabout. Like being terrified by a number on the scale in the morning and vowing never to overeat again, a shot of shame may get us through to lunch but never through to our freedom. Self-hatred, shame, and fear—though rampant in so many of our hidden worlds—are simply never going to be capable of creating or sustaining the growth we long for. Yet most women try to use shame as their inner motivator. I know I have.

Self-discipline isn't going to cut it either.

Discipline, particularly spiritual discipline, is a holy and good thing, one that increases over a lifetime of practice. But when we lean on it alone to bring about the change we long for, we find that the fruit is *not* a grace-filled woman. We get angry; we get discouraged. If we do make it through a few battles, we can easily become the kind of woman who pressures others to do the same, a hard and get-your-act-together kind of woman. With self-discipline, the focus remains "self," so we are already off to a bad start. Trying, striving, working harder may get us through the week, but it won't take us through the decades. Yet most Christian women believe that this is the way to handle our external world.

I got a kick out of an email I received last week:

> Some women at our church decided to do a study on the Proverbs 31 woman. I joined because I want to get to know these ladies, but really, I loathe the Proverbs 31 woman. She makes me feel like *&#@. But anyway, last week the study told us to buy a new mattress (so we sleep better, so we can serve more) and clean out our pantry, and yesterday it said I should only eat vegetables and water for the next 10 days (like Daniel), and today I'm supposed to stop eating sugar (and serving it to my family). I say to my husband, "So, we need a new mattress and we are going vegetarian and I'm cutting out all sugar from your diet and mine." He remarks: "No wonder you hate her!"

Now, some of those changes may be good things. Maybe God is calling her or us to do some of those things. But true transformation cannot be forced from the outside. It's an inside-out process. Who of us has not received or created a list of ways to live, eat, exercise, respond, seek God, grow, and change—and how long did it last, if it worked at all? Those lists don't work very long for *anyone*, and so we fall back into self-contempt. The problem does not lie with our lack of discipline. The problem is in the approach. The problem lies with the lists.

By the way, we humans are great ones for making lists. Codes of behavior. Rules of etiquette. Do not reapply your lipstick in public. Cover your mouth when you yawn. Wedding gifts can be sent up to a year after the event, but for heaven's sake, kindly let them know if you are attending or not. Keep your napkin on your lap. Don't talk while you are eating. Chew with your mouth closed. Come to a complete stop at a stop sign. Use your turn signals. Don't interrupt. Wait your turn. Stand up straight. Register to vote.

Aren't you tired just reading this?

God gave Israel a fabulous list. Do not lie. Do not steal. Do not covet your neighbor's wife, servant, ox, donkey, or new car. Was it really too much to ask? Noble as the list was, the people found they couldn't keep it for a day. Enter Jesus. In his famous Sermon on the Mount, Jesus taught that lusting after a woman (or man) *in your heart* was the same thing as committing adultery. He taught that hating a person *in your heart* was the same as murdering that person. Ummmm, we are all in trouble here.

A list of laws, rules, tips, techniques, and strategies does not a transformed heart make. No wonder 95 percent of all people who lose weight are unable to keep it off. Diet programs work. If you work the program. But they work from the outside in, and without substantive internal change, it's impossible to hold the ground of a lower BMI. Yes, we all have areas in our lives we want and need to change, but the only way that is going to happen is when we have a change of *heart*.

Scrooge had a change of heart, so he gave Bob Cratchit a raise. Cinderella had a change of heart, so she went to the ball. Raging Saul the Pharisee had a change of heart, so he became missionary number one for Jesus. I had a change of heart when I surrendered my life and gave it over to Jesus. When my heart came home to its true Home, a lot of change instantly happened.

When we have a change of heart on the inside, it manifests itself on the outside. But you and I both know by now that most of our healing and changing doesn't happen at the moment of our conversion. We walk it out. God invites us into a process. Our journey to get there takes place in the day in and day out of the dusty and gritty here and now. And it is to the dusty, gritty here and now that Jesus comes.

So shame isn't gonna do it, and discipline isn't gonna do it. God invites us to join him in the process whereby he heals our inner world so he can transform our outer world.

One more point before we explore how.

God is not going to love me any more or any differently when and if I finally lose this weight and become free from the stranglehold of food. Jesus's love for me, my Father's love for me, never changes. Yeah, okay, fellowship may be strained at times, but his heart toward me does not change. He is passionately in love with me. Even better, I think he likes me. And by the way, he's got a pretty huge thing for you, too. Yes, you. So what does being loved like that mean? Does that even matter? Does it make any difference in my day-to-day life? You bet it does.

we are loved

God has a thing for human beings. Though as you look around the planet, this does at times seem hard to believe, it remains true. We are loved. Born out of love, into love, to know love, and to be loved. Yes, we were born into a fallen, sorry world, which is at the same time more lovely than any fairy tale. It is both. And in this beautiful, heartbreaking world, God—the eternal, omniscient, amazing One—loves human beings. Including you. Especially you.

You are amazing.

Well, okay, maybe not every day. Every day the wonder of you is amazing, but many days the wonder of you is buried beneath the rubble of a world gone mad. You were born into a glorious mess, and we all have become something of a glorious mess ourselves. And in the midst of our mess, God has a thing for us. He does not despise our humanity or despair over our condition as we sometimes do. He does not turn his face away from us in our failings or our self-centeredness, as we would like to. He is not *surprised*. He is aware that we are but dust and our feet are made of clay, and he has made arrangements for us to not stay that way.

Let me say this truth again: you are loved. Deeply. Profoundly. Unimaginably loved. And you are a wondrous creature. Whether you can kill a spider or not. Whether the one-size-fits-all bathrobe swallows you or won't cover you. Whether you are having victory in every area of your life or not. Whether you just lost your temper (again) or indulged in a fantasy, another cookie, or thoughts of self-contempt. You are loved. Right here in this very moment, you are loved and pursued and seen by the One who sees everything. He knows you better than you know yourself, and you have never been a disappointment to him.

You are not disappointing him now. You may be disappointed, but he is not. Jesus knew what he was in for when he came "to seek and to save what was lost" (Luke 19:10). He came to seek and to save *all* that was lost—in our loving and living and dreaming and longing. He has saved us, and he is saving us still. We are being transformed into the very image of Christ. Whether we feel like it or not.

> And we, who with unveiled faces all reflect the Lord's glory, are being transformed into his likeness with ever-increasing glory, which comes from the Lord, who is the Spirit. (2 Cor. 3:18)

I know, I know—most days it sure doesn't feel like ever-increasing glory. It's a mess. And God is in the mess. He is about transforming our inner mess so he can transform the rest of the mess. Our transformation begins when we believe we are loved.

Jesus understands our struggles and our sorrows. He knows that our hearts have been broken, and he has come to heal them. He knows we long to change; he knows what needs to happen and where. He knows what is in the way. Though we are too much for ourselves, we are not too much for him.

Jesus will show us the way. Jesus is the Way. Which brings us to a shining paradox.

becoming

My friend Julie was being faithful to her new fitness regime. She went for her prescribed run even though it was raining. She felt like she was slogging along yet one more time when another runner passed her, leaping like a gazelle. *Maybe fitness is only for the fit*, she thought. *God!* she cried out, *change is so hard!* She heard his reply deep in her heart. *What if change is actually just me unveiling who you really are?*

Wait—what?

I thought we basically got rid of ourselves, one way or another, and Jesus sort of took over and lived our life for us. Didn't John the Baptist say, "He must become greater; I must become less" (John 3:30)?

This is the paradox of our change. On the one hand, it involves surrendering ourselves to God, giving everything over to him—including all our efforts to change and all our resignation that we'll never change. As C. S. Lewis said, "Until you have given up your self to Him you will not have a real self."[1]

And yet God does not then toss us aside. He restores us—the real us. As he heals our inner life, he calls us to rise to the occasion of our lives. Once we surrender ourselves, he gives us back our true selves. In fact, the most important journey any person will take is the journey into becoming herself through the love of God. It is a journey that will require courage, faith, and above all a willingness to grow and to let go. The journey of becoming is one of increased self-awareness coupled with a surrender of self.

God is all about this process of becoming. We come into this world brand-spanking new and begin the journey of becoming with our first breath. Breathing is good. Perhaps we should all take a deep breath now. Listen:

> The one who calls you is faithful and he will do it. (1 Thess. 5:24)

It is a beautiful paradox that the more *God's* we become, the more *ourselves* we become—the "self" he had in mind when he thought of you before the creation of the world. She's in there; she might be badly bruised and covered with all sorts of muck, but she's in there. And Jesus comes to call her out. The path is a dance between choosing and yielding, desiring and relinquishing, trying and giving up.

We discover as we grow that there are tools that are not helping us along our way toward change, but hurting us.

The voice of Shame says, *I basically hate me; I need to get rid of me.* The voice of Discipline says, *I've got to fix me, because me is not good.* God says, *I love you; let me restore you.* I like that one best.

God is *unveiling* who we truly are. Unveiled faces, as Paul put it. All those veils of shame and sin and the false self, all those veils others have put upon us, thinking they know who we ought to be—God takes them all away so that with unveiled faces we might reflect his glory.

The process often feels slow, interminable even. But lasting change takes time. Anyone can muscle through a day; New Year's resolutions may even last a few months. But God is a God of process, and he has his eye on eternity. His plans for us aren't for a quick fix but an eternal transformation. Slowly. Carefully. Intentionally. The unveiling is taking place.

So—is there a way to speed up the process of unveiling and hasten the change we long for?

Yes. There is. Accelerating our "becoming" involves saying yes to God again and again and again. It is not a posture of striving but of releasing. It looks a lot more like yielding than pushing through to the next goal. We collapse into God's life within us. "Christ in me, help me" becomes our prayer. That is why he often brings us to the end of our ropes, the end of ourselves. Because it is from there we turn from our striving and raise our arms in surrender to our God *again* to save us.

By faith, we turn to him. By faith, we choose to believe that he hears our prayer. By faith, we believe he is good and is for us. By faith, we trust that though we may not see it or feel it, God is at work in us and for us. Because he says he is.

together

Does anybody ever really change? I believe they do. I've seen it happen; the Scriptures promise it can happen; it's happening in me.

God has come for me, and he continues to come for me. He has healed me, and he continues to heal me. He has saved me, and he is saving me still, crafting his beauty and presence more deeply into my soul. "I Am" has taken up residence, and his very presence is changing me. He who is utterly himself is enabling me to become myself, the self he had in mind when he made me.

Think of it—God is completely himself and at peace with that fact. Isn't that what the large creature walking alongside Shasta says to him in that wonderful tale *The Horse and His Boy*? Disheartened Shasta asks the Voice next to him, "Who *are* you?" Though it is the great lion, he does not reply, "I am Aslan." Like Yahweh, he simply answers, "Myself."[2] He is who he is, who he has always been, and who he will always be. God is *I Am*. He is not becoming. He already is. And now, because of him, I too am becoming *myself*.

Sure, I still tend to replay conversations I've had with others in my head, looking for my mistakes, but I linger in self-contempt less these days. Yes, I still reach for carbohydrates when the only thing hungry is my soul, but I do it less often. I am growing in knowing that I am completely loved in this moment and that God isn't waiting for me to get my act together in order to become worthy of his affection. I have lost some weight. The one-size-fits-all bathrobe does fit me now. But I know that I do not possess more of God's approval because of it. I am not more qualified as a Christian. I am no more beautiful to him than I have ever been. I have only and ever been lovely to God, and so have you. In the steady face of his love, I am changing. I am becoming myself.

I know you have tried to change and hoped for change in the past. Today, God is inviting you to hope again. By *faith*. We cannot heal ourselves or free ourselves or save ourselves. We cannot become ourselves all by ourselves. But we are not by ourselves. We are seen and known and strengthened and urged on to the life we were created for by the King of Love. He wants to help us to become. He wants to help us change and grow. We can't do it, but *he can*. He's very, very good at it. It is, in fact, what he has promised to do.

> For God knew his people in advance, and he chose them to become like his Son, so that his Son would be the firstborn among many brothers and sisters. (Rom. 8:29 NLT)

Here is what I've learned:

> Spiders are really ugly, but most of them cannot kill you.
> We are loved beyond telling.
> There are *reasons* why we struggle with the things we do.
> And there is a way to become the woman God meant us
> to be.

Let's explore that process together.

2

looking back with mercy

It doesn't matter who my father was; it matters who I remember he was.
—Anne Sexton, "A Small Journal," *The Poet's Story*

I wish my life came with a do-over button.

If only I knew then what I know now! If only I had just kept my mouth shut! Why did I do that, say that, want *that*? Still, I realize the reason I am where I am is because of the journey I have been on. And not just the lovely "I'd love to do that again" parts of my journey either. The ugly parts, too. I got here from there. I would love to change much of my story and particularly the times when my struggles and failures have caused my family and friends grief.

But God is in their stories as well, and so with an open hand, surrounded by grace, my only option is to learn and begin again. Remember and step forward. Forgetting my life—my mistakes, my victories, my challenges, my sorrows, my *story*—prevents me from moving forward and growing into the woman I am supposed to be. I must remember. I invite you to join me in remembering. It may seem strange that at certain points on our journey we need to look back in order to continue moving forward, but it's true.

The temptation is to look back with regret rather than with mercy. But God's eyes see clearly, and they are filled with mercy. We can be merciful too.

It's not that I remember everything clearly. It comes to me unbidden, my history, in a fragrance I catch on the breeze, in the sound of the birds happily going about their joyous business of finding things to eat. It is a hint of eternity on the wind, a connection to seasons past, the memory of wonder, of longing, of *knowing*. I am still three and seven and twenty-two.

at five and forty-nine

When I was a child of five, my family took a vacation to the Grand Teton National Park. We stayed in a lodge made up of separate log cabins, and we had a stream flowing behind our little house. I was Pocahontas and Audra Barkley and Laura Ingalls Wilder all at once and utterly, gloriously myself.

My brother caught a fish, and the lodge chef grilled it up for him for dinner. My sisters went horseback riding while my brother, my parents, and I took a float trip down the Snake River. The shifting waters lulled me to sleep, and I napped on the bottom of the raft in the warmth of the sun. We hiked up Jenny Lake trail and we swam in Jackson Lake and we kept our bottles of Coca-Cola freezing cold by tying them to a log in the lake.

It was a golden time, a time that has shone in my dreams and in my memory. We were explorers and adventurers, and we were free and happy. It was good. *We* were good. It was a holy reprieve from an unholy life.

Our very first afternoon there, we rolled up our pants and waded into the river behind the cabin in the bracing water. My mother laughed as she caught me before I was swept downstream, saving my life as only a mother does a thousand times a childhood. Clear waters. Pristine moments. Cherished memories.

Now I return year after year to the Tetons with my own children, and it feels like coming home, a God-filled beauty that is unchanged (though my own reflection is not). I love this place of memory and hope where the landscape echoes of what should always have been.

I spent years searching for the particular log cabin my family stayed in, and at the age of forty-nine I found it. My husband pulled into the parking lot, and I got out of the car alone, leaving him and my bewildered children to wait as I stepped back in time.

No longer a guest lodge but cabins that house the American Alpine Climbers Club, the buildings are not well kept and ruggedly lovely but as used and rundown as my heart sometimes feels. I walk to the end of the lot to where our cabin was. There it stands. The time spent there was real. I check myself. *If it is this place and this cabin, then there will be a stream flowing behind.* Expectant yet guarded, I walk to the back. The river is flowing high now. There is no safe wading at this time of year, but there it is—wild, clear, clean. Water rushing over stones.

I am keenly aware of the sound of the water and of the wind in the trees above me, and then I am aware of another sound. Laughter. The laughter of children and the laughter of a woman—the laughter of my mother. It's not in my imagination, nor in my present moment, but it's as real as my breath. Laughter reaches out to me from a place closer than the breeze that brushes my face. The light doesn't change, the fragrance is the same, but a window into eternity has opened—and the sound is heavenly: free, joyous, true *laughter.*

I linger in the moment, realizing that at forty-nine years old I am fifteen years older than my mother was when she grasped my floating body as I passed her, catching me with joyous ease. It has been ten years since I have heard my mother's laugh. She is dead. I know this to be true. I was there. I witnessed her passing, her spirit releasing and her body quickly following. But now, in this moment, I hear her laughter, the laughter of a young woman whose life in this moment is good.

My mother is dead. My mother is alive.

My mother is gone. My mother remains.

I am forty-nine years old. And I am three and I am seven and I am twenty-two.

At times there is within me an echo of the truth that I am eternal. I am connected to my present, my future, my past. So are you. We carry within us every age and every moment of our lives.

> *The great thing about getting older is that you*
> *don't lose all the other ages you've been.*
> —Madeleine L'Engle

remembering honestly

It's important to remember. For me, the soundtrack of my childhood is crickets and thunderstorms and the sound of autumn leaves crunching beneath my feet and releasing their earthy fragrance. I grew up in a neighborhood without fences and filled with children. We explored "the ditch." We caught fireflies and put them in a mason jar. Really. We did this. It isn't just in the movies. We played Red Rover, Red Rover and Starlight, Star Bright and put on musicals for our parents.

There were four seasons, with ice skating on a real frozen lake in the winter and swimming in the public pool all summer long. We carved pumpkins at Halloween and went trick or treating unescorted, safe to go into a stranger's home to get our picture taken. There were lemonade stands and sledding, tornado drills and bike riding, Sunday mass and come-home snacks.

At six years old, while I was sick in bed with the chickenpox, I got the news I had won a newspaper coloring contest. What joy! I still have the photo my mother took when she told me of my victory. I'm smiling, sitting up next to my Pebbles doll, missing teeth on prominent display. My prize was a gift certificate to a candy store and the thrill of being chosen. Oh yes. I remember.

My mother made dinner for us every night. Every single night. Dinners out as a family were a rare extravagance reserved for New Year's Eve and the occasional road trip. "How much money can we spend?" we asked as we poured over the mystery of the menu. My mother didn't wear pearls, but she did wear an apron. And if she wasn't playing bridge, volunteering at the church, or cleaning the house, she could be found in our kitchen.

Most days, after coming home from school, I parked myself in front of the television. *Father Knows Best. The Rifleman.* I can still sing jingles from commercials that are forty years old. I don't remember having a lick of homework. My, have things changed.

When I was thirty-five years old, the mother of three sons myself and married for eleven years, both my husband and I were in counseling. Separately. I began a year before he did, and I finished (that round) a year after him. When he came home one day and told me that his counselor had declared that season in my husband's life over—that he had graduated from counseling—I was stunned. What was the deal with that? I asked him, "How come you're finished with counseling in such a short time when *your* family was such a bigger mess than mine?" He looked me straight in the eyes and answered, "It's because you think so, that's why."

Wait. What? My childhood was awesome. What was he suggesting? Was he saying that my childhood was perhaps not the idyllic *Ozzie and Harriet* show I remembered? I felt the earth shift beneath my feet as I considered this long shot of a possibility.

It's important to remember. But it's also very important to remember *honestly*. (At least when we are ready and equipped by God to do so.)

When I am honest, the soundtrack of my childhood is also the clink of ice cubes and the smell of scotch. It is the sound of barbed words flung between my parents with deadly accuracy and belts being snapped in preparation for a spanking. It is the numbing dullness wafting from the television and the sound of beer cans being opened. It is the feeling of an anxious stomach, a lonely heart, and the unfulfilled desire to be played with. It is the tangible ache of wanting to be accepted, approved of, and enjoyed. It is the sense of failing miserably.

In the ongoing remembering of my own story, God is revealing reality. It's been a journey into loss and sorrow and intense pain. It has included becoming very angry. And slowly, ever so slowly, but ever so surely, it has involved mercy, forgiveness, healing, and love.

My childhood was not idyllic. Since no one's was, I'm guessing it's a pretty safe bet yours wasn't either. But a deeper understanding of our stories leads to a deeper understanding of ourselves—who we are and who God has made us to be. Yes, there is sorrow there, but there is glory, too.

shaped by childhood

The first ten years of a person's life pass all too quickly, but the effect of them colors the rest of life. Whether mostly good or mostly awful, most women's childhoods are a mixture of both. They are meant to be years free and unencumbered by weighty adult issues. These are the wonder years, the years of blowing bubbles, drawing on the sidewalk with chalk, and finding whales in the clouds. Marked by exploration, the sound of swing sets, and the smell of dandelions, these formative years are the foundation of the women we are today.

Do you remember what you were like? What *you* liked? What games you enjoyed? Were *you* enjoyed?

The youngest of five daughters, Annie grew up in rural Minnesota, surrounded by open space and extended family. Her blonde hair and blue eyes fit right in with her Dutch sisters, but her weak and ill little body did not. Annie had severe asthma that prevented her from participating in sports or neighborhood pickup games of soccer. Gripped by unrelenting fear at bedtime, she spent most nights on her parents' bedroom floor. The allergies that plagued her kept her from gaining weight and breathing deeply and living with abandon. Annie describes her little girl self as sickly, skinny, and lonely.

How do athletic parents devoted to their active children convey love and approval to an unathletic, sickly, uninvolved child? Annie did not grow up feeling enjoyed. She did not fit into her family. Annie felt that her parents didn't know what to do with her, so they didn't do anything. Left to herself more often than not, one of the defining wounds of her life came from the hands of a cousin. Left unattended and unprotected for hours upon hours, Annie was sexually abused. As is the story with too many women (and men), the effect of being violated was that Annie believed she was not worth protecting, not worth attending to, not really worth anything at all. There is something wrong with me, she believed.

What was your childhood like? What do you remember even now? What did you love, dream of, play, feel, believe? Invite Jesus into your memory and into your perception of it.

Memory makes it possible for us both to bless the past, even those parts of it that we have always felt cursed by, and also to be blessed by it.
—Frederick Buechner, *Telling Secrets*

be more, be less

My siblings and I used to torture each other in tickle fights. Not play—torture. I have two sisters and one brother, and I am the youngest, so both my experience and my memory of my childhood vary vastly from theirs. We get together these days and share stories that we remember very differently. I was ten years old when my father stopped drinking; my brother was fourteen, my sisters sixteen and seventeen. A few years later my father was diagnosed with bipolar disorder and began to take the medicine that stabilized his emotions. But by that time, my sisters had left home and my brother had left in every other way he could. So like I said, their experience of childhood varies much from my own. But I do know that in the tickle fights, whoever was pinned to the ground would be tickled until they couldn't breathe and usually with a damp sponge gagging their mouth. Or perhaps a dirty sock.

Why do we do these things?

We had a family song. If we got together this afternoon, my siblings and I could sing it to you in perfect harmony: "It Was Only an Old Beer Bottle." Now what does that tell you about our family? I will tell you that whoever opened my father's beer can was rewarded with the first sip. At three years old I vied for the privilege. I still like the taste of it.

> *It was only an old beer bottle,*
> *A-floating on the foam.*
> *It was only an old beer bottle,*
> *A million miles from home.*
> *And in it was a message*
> *With these words written on:*
> *Whoever finds this bottle*
> *Will find the beer all gone. (Beeeeer allllll gooooone.)*

So we were a singing family. Sort of. And though I am confident of my siblings' love for me, growing up we weren't exactly allies. We weren't enemies either. Our alliances shifted. (Except for Terri, my oldest sister. All of us, even my parents, could count on Terri. She was mercy, the peacemaker, the steadying factor in our family, the one who would keep searching for my glasses long after I had given up.)

Still, though we lived together and felt the same unspoken threat of impending disaster, we were alone. Alone in the way we coped with the mess of our parents' marriage and the message we were each given: *you are a profound disappointment in who you are.* You need to, why can't you—the list is endless. Weigh less. Be more tan. Be more athletic. Be more involved. Be popular. Play sports. Play golf. Play the piano. Be more. Be less. Be *different.*

diets

The first diet my mother put me on was when I was in the fourth grade. I was eight years old and a wee bit chubby. School lunches (and thank you that you made them at all, Mom) from that age on consisted of celery sticks and Buddig lunch meat. Oh for those lucky ones who got the little bags of potato chips or—bliss—a Hostess something in their lunches!

I lost the seven pounds I needed to lose with much praise and applause, and there you have it. Studies show that if you put a person on a low-calorie diet regime, they will lose a few pounds, yes. But their bodies will acclimate to the regime, and they will struggle to varying degrees with keeping their weight in a normal range from then on. Diet to lose weight, and you get hooked.

My father's work was in the fashion industry. Uh-oh. His wife and his daughters' appearance, as well as his son's, was paramount. My mother had a fabulous figure. She never believed it, was constantly on one diet or another, and tried to "help" her daughters too. Intent on my being thin, my parents sent me to a dietician when I was in the tenth grade. I had to keep a log of what I ate, learn about nutrition, and weigh in every week. I was fifteen years old. I was five feet, seven inches tall. I weighed 140 pounds.

I look at pictures of me growing up, bracing myself to see the fat, homely girl I was, and there looking back at me is a pretty, unsure of herself, but totally normal-weighing little girl. What was the deal? By some grace of God I didn't become anorexic or bulimic, but I did seek comfort in food. Though for many years, only a little. The secret extra four cookies, from the freezer so Mom wouldn't notice.

My mother wanted me to be more than she thought I was, more than she thought *she* was. Who we both were, clearly, was not enough. And too much.

Mom, looking at my hair askance: "Jenny wears her hair so stylishly, you don't even notice that *she's* overweight." Wallis Simpson's mantra, "A woman can never be too rich or too thin," was gospel. At least the thin part. The less you weigh, the more value you have.

As I sought solace for my heart in promiscuity my last two years of high school, my weight began to rise. Fifteen pounds in high school might as well have been fifty. So I had my two years of being truly overweight. Miserable. When I went off to college I discovered the power of amphetamines, and in two months lost more weight than I needed to lose. But I still saw myself as the "fat girl." Unwanted. Unattractive. Ready to tip the scale into rejection at any moment. I felt I was a disappointment to my parents, never able to attain an unspoken but deeply felt level of acceptance. I and my siblings never felt we measured up.

And God was there.

God was there

My family moved from Kansas to California when I was ten years old, and thirty years later I had the opportunity to go back. As I drove slowly to the old neighborhood, I asked God to show me that he had been there for me. Pulling up in front of my well-remembered, well-loved childhood home, he answered. There, standing guard on the front porch, was a large statue of a lion. The Lion of Judah whispered to my heart that he had been standing guard the entire time. I parked the car and walked up the street to my elementary school. It was there that a few teachers had singled me out in their attention and nourished my famished heart.

"I know you were here, God. But can you show me?" The school had become a church. I was able to walk in and down the hall to my last classroom. I peeked in the windows, and there on the board, written as big as life, were the words, "God loves you."

Oh yeah, he was there.

He was there for Annie, too. When she was thirty years old, God invited Annie to remember. And remember she did. She remembered her sorrow, her loneliness, her pain. And then she remembered something else. As a little girl, Annie loved the springtime. When winter would finally release its grip on her world, Annie would put on her boots and head out to the swamp near her home. It wasn't full of quicksand, but it was filled with mud. At the first sign of spring it was filled with something else as well. Buttercups. Pale yellow, tender, intricate, tiny proclaimers of beauty, buttercups would cover the swamp in wonder. A simple flower, buttercups bestow their loveliness only to muddy swamps. Buttercups do not grow in fields of fertilized grasslands. They do not display their presence on country hillsides. They only flourish in mud.

Annie's childhood was muddy. And honestly, she is one of the most beautiful women I have ever been privileged to know. Beauty for ashes. Praise for despair. The phoenix rises, and Annie has risen too with a faith that is precious and contagious and lovely beyond words. She is Jesus's very own Buttercup. Yes, God was there. He is still there.

Annie's childhood was muddy, and so was mine. There were times when yours was too. And God was there for you, too. Calling. Providing.

Shielding. Aching. Loving. Why did he allow certain things to happen? I don't know. We won't know until we get to ask him face-to-face. But we do know that he is good and he is for us.

Paul writes, "And we know that in all things God works for the good of those who love him, who have been called according to his purpose" (Rom. 8:28). One day we will understand completely. For this moment, though, we are being invited to see with his eyes of mercy.

Why don't you ask him about your younger years? Ask him to show you in some creative way that your heart will understand if and how he was there.

what did we do with it?

Every human being has some vital place in their life where they are not living in the victory they long for, and it colors how they view themselves. Every woman's personal struggle rooted in her past, be it fear of intimacy or a deep-rooted self-hatred or a pressing need to control her world, makes her desperate for God. We all have something that brings us to our knees. It isn't something we would ever choose for ourselves or wish on anyone else, but we all have an area or ten in our lives that drives us to need God. We can't free ourselves. We are weak, aware that something inside is broken and starving. It is a wonderful grace when we finally give up and fall down before the One who is strong.

And my friend, it is not a bad thing that you desperately need Jesus. For some reason, we feel embarrassed by our desperation; we see desperation as a sign that something is terribly wrong with us. Oh no. We were created to desperately need Jesus. We have always needed him, and we always will. I do not believe God "caused" the pain of our lives, but I do know that he uses it to drive us to himself. The desperation is a good thing. As George MacDonald wrote,

How many helps Thou giv'st to those would learn!
To some sore pain, to others a sinking heart;
To some a weariness worse than any smart;
To some a haunting, fearing, blind concern ...
To some a hunger that will not depart.[1]

I am a hungry woman. I am hungry for love, for acceptance, for belonging, for meaning. I am desperate for God. I am aware of the aching abyss inside me of which many have written. Oswald Chambers wrote, "There is only One being who can satisfy the last aching abyss of the human heart, and that is the Lord Jesus Christ."[2] I know that now. But I certainly didn't know it as a little girl hungry for approval and love. I didn't wake every morning knowing that Jesus is the one who will satisfy the starving places in my heart. I have grown into knowing it. I continue to grow into knowing it.

I wasn't even aware of how hungry I was when as a newlywed I first began to give my heart away to the drive-thru. I didn't know I was making a deal with bondage. Food would satisfy my hunger, my loneliness, my ache for a while. But only for a little while. And then I would need another fix. I would get another fix, and then I got into a fix that I have spent the better part of thirty years trying to get out of.

The messages I received growing up, and particularly my mother's fixation on my weight, set me up for the struggle. The way had been paved for food to hold a power in my life it was never meant to. Obsession with the number on the scale and the size of the clothes turned over the measurement of my value as a woman to my weight and appearance.

My bondage to binging has shaped my life as profoundly as any other thing or person. What I came to believe about myself through my helpless state (failure) and how I chose to fight through my shame and still show up and offer what I could to others shaped my soul. Witnessing the way my husband's heart was broken and transformed through *my* losing battle with food is a massively defining part of my story. A large portion of it. An extra large portion of it. (Yes, I get the pun.)

toward healing

In my anguish and despair, I hit my knees and turn my face to Jesus again and again and again. My cries for help have been agonizing groans laden with self-loathing, accusation, and desperation. And God has met me. In the midst of overwhelming shame not merely over my body but my *self*, God has drawn me to his heart and spoken to me Truth. He speaks Love and Truth, right in the middle of my pain and the familiar voices screaming my failure.

Part of our healing comes with forgiveness (of ourselves and others), and part of it comes with repentance. But first, we have to begin with how God sees us. How he sees *you*. Do you know?

> You are deeply and completely loved (Rom. 8:38–39).
> You are totally and completely forgiven (1 John 2:12).
> When God sees you, he sees the righteousness of Jesus
>   (2 Cor. 5:21).
> You mean the whole world to him (John 3:16).
> He thinks you are beautiful. Right now (Song 4:1).
> He is committed to your restoration (Rom. 8:29).
> You are not now, nor have you ever been, alone
>   (Heb. 13:5).

I have lost weight over the past few years, in a healthy way. But before God ever changed my body, he changed the way I saw myself. He took me back into my story, back into those wounds, and he helped me to renounce the lies spoken over me. He helped me to forgive, both those who hurt me and also myself. This is how God brings about change—from the inside out. From our hearts. This is the journey we will take together in this book. Oh sister, there is so much more God has for you.

Let me say a word or two more about forgiveness. Forgiveness is crucial if we are to look back in mercy at our stories. Forgiveness, like repentance, is essential and always our choice. But in order to forgive, we need to know what we are forgiving.

My husband's father was an alcoholic for many, many years. When he was drinking, he was a dangerous man. He did untold damage to his family, but his cruelty was particularly aimed at one of John's sisters. John's father stopped drinking after his children were off and married and raising their own children. More importantly, his father repented of the hurt his alcoholism caused, and John and he had many good conversations before he passed away in 2011. There is complete forgiveness and the certainty of a reunion in heaven, but like many alcoholics, John's father did not remember what he was like or what he did when he was drunk.

About fifteen years ago, in an effort to restore relationship with his children, John's father wrote them all a letter asking for their forgiveness. In it he said, "I don't remember what I did, but I'm sorry." He was saying that perhaps he had done some things, maybe many things wrong, but he didn't know what they were. John's sister's response was, "He can't remember what I can never forget." The apology lacked weight. But forgiveness does not wait on an apology. It still remains a choice.

My struggle with obesity is only a part of my story. Yes, it is a large part and frames more than two decades of my life, but God has used it to draw my heart to himself. I don't believe he has caused it. But I know that he has used it. And I choose to forgive my mother. I forgive my father. I even forgive myself. Again.

rewriting my story

God is rewriting my story. My story is *his* story, really, and one day he will tell it in all of its hidden splendor. I will get to hear his take on my days, his perception on what was going on underneath and behind the scenes. He will share with me the many ways he was working all things together for my good, and it will be marvelous to hear. One day he will tell you your story, too. And it will be glorious. God has been loving me, shielding me, and he has been doing the same for you. Though perhaps we do not see it yet as clearly as we one day will.

I have begun remembering long-forgotten things these last few years. Memories are surfacing of being loved and enjoyed by both my mother and my father. The debris of loss and sorrow is being swept away by mercy and forgiveness and the love of God, and in their place comes love revealed.

One Christmas, my dad came home from a trip and brought me a plastic blowup Rudolph. This red-nosed reindeer was just for me. I can see my dad bending down to give it to me and feel the joy in me rise as he did. He gave me a little black plastic stuffed dog. The dog smelled like pepper, so I named him Pepper. He was precious to me for many years and remained precious even after my dog ate his ears off.

I remember other little gifts. Other small and large acts of kindness. My father gave me things unexpectedly as a sign of his love for me. How did I miss that? I am not missing it now.

I understand these days that when my visiting mother would look at me askance and say, "Let me take you bra shopping," she was actually loving me. For most of our years together, we didn't speak the same language, so too often our offerings of love were missed. But I am not missing them now. She heard my starfish story (I wrote about it in *Captivating*) and gave me a starfish Christmas ornament later that year. I cherish it. She saved some of my baby clothes and entrusted them to me with the words, "You were so precious." She gave my husband the "permission" to ask me to marry him (my father had died the year before) with the words, "Stasi is special. She has always been special." And now I can remember her saying those same words to me many, many, *many* times.

Let God begin to rewrite your story. Invite him to show you your past through his eyes. Ask him to surface good memories you have forgotten. He would love to do it. There is healing to be had there. There is a replacing of regret with mercy.

Though our past has shaped us, we are not our past. Though our failures and sin have had an effect on who we are, we are not defined by our failures or our sin. Though thought patterns and addictions have overwhelmed us, we are not overcome by them and we will never be overcome by them. Jesus has won our victory. Jesus is our victory.

The stories from our past that shaped us and the words that were spoken over our lives that have crippled us do not stand a chance in the light of the powerful grace and mercy that come to us now in the Person of Jesus. We do not have to remain captive any longer. Yes, God uses our stories to shape us. He works all things for the good of those who love him, even the horrible things. The holy work of God deep in our hearts as we have suffered and struggled and wept and longed to overcome is stunning beyond measure. You may not see the goodness yet, but you will. You will. It comes when we see our lives through God's eyes.

God is coming. He has not abandoned us, and he never will. Yes, the pain of life is sometimes too intense to be borne. But when from that place we cry out to Jesus to save us, the heavens rejoice, the demons tremble in defeat, and the Holy Spirit who is closer than our skin transforms us.

Jesus is inviting us to recover those parts of ourselves we have tried to hide or lop off in hopes of being more acceptable. God wants us to love him with all of our hearts. God has purchased all our freedom with his blood. Including the portions of our personalities we would like to change, the dreams long buried, and the wounds we have ignored. They are being kissed awake by the Holy Spirit. Come alive, my Beloved. Awaken. Remember. Jesus has come to heal us and restore us to himself, to others, and even to ourselves.

3

the landscape of our lives

What lies behind us and what lies before us are tiny matters compared to what lies within us.
—Ralph Waldo Emerson

Driving to a meeting yesterday, I passed a young woman in a minivan who looked lost. She lingered at the stop sign far too long, looking one way, then the other. In the brief moment that I saw her face, I glimpsed both uncertainty and profound discomfort with being uncertain. Frozen in her tracks, she might have been frozen in time, for she was me twenty years ago. In my early thirties, I too was lost. I longed for approval but was certain of disapproval. I hoped to be enjoyed and not found lacking, but I felt unenjoyable and completely lacking. Somewhere, somehow, I felt I had missed the course on managing life.

Yes, I knew that the Bible says the God of the universe sings over me symphonies of delight. But my life experiences and self-loathing had rendered me deaf to his voice.

As we journey on in our becoming, we all get lost now and then. It is essential that we look up from the road and determine where we are, take note of our surroundings, check for mile markers. Context explains so much. Sure, we all lose our bearings, lose even ourselves, but we don't want to *remain* lost. So I'd like to try and describe for you the setting of our lives as women. Did you know that there even *is* a setting, a landscape we all must navigate? This will be mighty helpful to you. Much of what you have been blaming on yourself has not been you at all. Every woman's journey has two realties we must know and navigate—one internal, the other external.

the mystery of hormones

Yesterday morning I wanted to buy a puppy; this afternoon I wondered how many years I would get for homicide.

Am I simply nuts? Is this just the sin nature the Bible talks about, and I'm stuck with repenting of it again and again? No, my dear sister. There is an internal reality playing havoc with my world, but it is neither woundedness, nor sin, nor immaturity—not even a touch of insanity. There are powerful feminine tides washing to and fro inside each of us, and they are having an enormous influence on our lives—and on the way we *perceive* our lives.

Until the late 1900s the average life expectancy of women was forty-eight years. Most women didn't live to experience the upheaval of menopause (though many lived in perimenopause, the difficult transition period that precedes it). Today, the average life expectancy for women is between seventy and eighty years. Most of us will not only experience menopause, we'll go on to live a good twenty to thirty years after crossing into it.

Research regarding hormones and women's bodies is relatively young but vastly increasing. Since women are living longer, there are more of us around asking for help and more professionals in the field taking us seriously. (You would have thought that men would have delved into this mystery long ago out of a sense of self-preservation.)

Women suffering from painful PMS or any hormonal imbalance used to be deemed merely emotional, hysterical, or unstable. Too many women today remain unaware of how their hormones are affecting their lives—emotionally, physically, and spiritually. But we don't need to remain uninformed any longer or wonder if at certain times in our lives (or a month) we are simply going crazy. The bodies we live in and the amazing hormones that shift and flow through them help set the stage of our experience of our lives. They contribute profoundly to the landscape of our personal histories and our present realities.

four seasons

The bodies of women mirror nature. Every year we have spring, summer, autumn, and winter—four necessary seasons that will continue until the end of our time. And just as winter sometimes makes itself at home smack dab in the middle of a glorious spring week, so does springtime beauty leak into winter for a brief respite. There are four seasons, but they bleed into one another. In the same way, there are four seasons (menstrually speaking) in a woman's life and four weeks to her cycle, but they are not always neatly separated. Some women's cycles are as irregular as an unscrupulous politician's voting record, and some women's cycles function like a Swiss clock. Either way, there is much benefit for us in understanding what is going on in our bodies.

Let's start with the four seasons. We have preadolescence when our child's body develops at a rapid and sometimes awkward rate. These years set the foundation of our self-perception. Our heart's deepest questions are being answered in these years. Am I loved? Am I worth loving? Am I captivating? From infants to toddlers to little girls, we are becoming our-selves, developing into the women we are today. In this season, we are fully feminine and are not yet encumbered (or blessed) by our period.

The next season of a woman's life is the season of menses, the decades of possessing the (theoretical) ability to bear a child. Entering into this season is characterized by massive hormonal changes. It can be a difficult transi-tion that often includes weight gain, breakouts, and titanic inner struggles. *Who am I? What makes me valuable? Where do I fit in?* Adolescence is *hard*. All the hormones being released into our bodies can make it an emotionally volatile time. Questions in our hearts continue to be answered as we settle into what becomes our womanhood. Our monthly period may be regular or come only as a complete surprise, but these years make up the longest season of a woman's life.

The incredible capacity given to women to bring forth life carries with it a staggering honor and a high price. This is the season where most women find themselves with every period coming either as a relief or a sort of death.[1]

The third season of a woman's life is known as perimenopause. During this season, which lasts up to a decade, our bodies change in ways as dra-matic as when we first entered into puberty.[2] For some lucky women it goes by practically unnoticed, but for many it can be agonizing. For most women, the experience falls somewhere in between. It is characterized by irregular bleeding, strong emotions, and relationships that may need to be renegotiated. Trouble sleeping falls here. Hot flashes begin here. And researchers have determined that hot flashes, previously thought to last one to two years, can last up to ten—lucky us! Oy. (I think I had my first one yesterday. I didn't know for sure because it's all new to me, but since I had to peel off layers of clothes, including my socks, and strip down to a light T-shirt and flip-flops to get comfortable, I hear it may have been one. Oh, and it's fifteen degrees outside, so maybe.)

For women with children, this may also be the season when the children begin leaving home. The timing of the empty nest coincides with the slow shutting off of the oh-so-helpful mothering hormones. We begin to have thoughts more often like, Make your own *&%@ dinner, or maybe we say it. We begin to remember what we wanted to learn and become when we were young and not sidetracked by taking care of others. It's a wonderful thing to have nourished our own gifting and desires throughout our lives, but if we have sacrificed parts of ourselves to tend to others (and who hasn't?), this is the time when we come back to our own becoming. God's timing in all of it is amazing.

The fourth season of a woman's life is called menopause, when we no longer have menstrual cycles, we can no longer get pregnant, and we don't need to worry about staining our pants. Many women live twenty to thirty years in what is sometimes called post-menopause. This season of life can be a marvelous one, with women stepping into a fuller expression of themselves. Creativity soars. Desires laid aside in the interest of raising a family resurface with vigor. Self-doubt and self-editing no longer hold the power they may have held when we were younger and less assured, and many women come to enjoy a previously unknown depth of self-appreciation. This is a really wonderful season.

The good news is that with God, we don't have to wait until we reach menopause in order to be a woman whose soul is at peace with who she is, free from the burden of other people's opinions and offering her unique and God-given strength.

life in a month

I'll just go ahead and admit that my favorite week of my menstrual cycle is the first one. I have energy and a positive attitude. I make plans to throw a party, exercise with gusto, and believe all the fabulous things God says about me in the Bible with more fervor than I did just a few days ago. Come on over and we'll bake a cake and then we'll take it to a homeless shelter. Yeah, baby.

My hormones are doing their life-bringing thing. I would like to believe that this version of myself is the truest me, but I'll still be me in three weeks when the party guests begin to arrive and I don't want them coming over to my house anymore. It's all me. The ups and downs, the highs and lows—and it's all you, too.

There are four weeks in a woman's cycle. Twenty-eight days. In the first week, estrogen is released and our ovaries begin work on an egg cell. Estrogen also helps to release other marvelous things in our brains like dopamine and serotonin. We are happier. Our energy level is at its highest, and if our husband winks at us before bedtime, we are very likely to wink back. Or wink first. This is our "You go, girl!" week.

When the second week begins, things change. Estrogen levels off and then declines. We are still energetic, strong, and creative, just perhaps not so manic. Then ovulation occurs. Estrogen rises slightly, and progesterone increases. The egg travels down the fallopian tube in anticipation of a chance encounter. ("Love was just a glance away, a warm embracing dance away."[3]) We are more peaceful inside and also perhaps more sexually assertive. But then our energy begins to lessen. Our emotions may become a bit conflicted.

In the third week, if no embryo was fertilized, our brains signal estrogen and progesterone to vacate the building. Emotions slide a little bit. Blood sugar levels slide too. We aren't feeling our confident selves as easily. For a few days, the empty space created by the departing hormones leaves many women feeling empty as well. This is not the ideal time to have a large gathering in your home.

Sometime during the fourth week, if we aren't pregnant, both estrogen and progesterone leave, and so does the endometrial lining that formed in our uterus to prepare a cozy place for an embryo. Our period begins.

Chocolate is irresistible. Commercials make us weepy. This is when we may wish we could unplug the phone and unplug from our life for a couple of days. These are the days to allow ourselves to slow down, take an afternoon nap, journal. A bubble bath may sound mighty nice. And then the crocus blooms. The daffodils make their happy appearance. Spring comes again, and hope rises. The cycle begins again.

See, you're not crazy! My menstrual cycles are ending, and I am just beginning to learn about them. Cycles have affected my moods for forty years, and just now I am learning that mood fluctuations are normal. I've felt crazy. Broken. Dismissable. Why didn't I chart them week by week before? (Dear sister, if you haven't practiced this, please chart your cycle. Make notes in your calendar each month so you know where you are. Look up, and take note of the signposts. You're not lost; you're in your third week, that's all.)

I have tried to live apart from my body, ignoring its cries for tending. I have tried to live apart from my emotions, ignoring their pleas for attention. It has not been a good choice. I've been living disconnected from my very self. I am my body just as much as I am my spirit, my soul, my emotions, my dreams, my desires, and my sense of humor. So honestly, right at this moment, I am not ignoring my very self. I will confess that I am low, tired, and my breasts feel heavy and sore. And because of what I've learned, I now know that this does not mean I am:

> Depressed
> Lost
> Confused
> Overwhelmed
> Nuts
> Making no headway
> Moody
> Forever stuck

It means my estrogen and progesterone are low. That's all. Isn't that a relief?

I am choosing to pray, asking Jesus to help me be kind to myself and to others, to allow myself to be tired and low. This is a normal part of being a woman. And yes, I do like the other weeks of the month much better. In my I-can-do-it-all week I want to write, speak, minister, experience more of the Holy Spirit, bring Jesus's healing, and paint a room. Today I don't want any of that. I want hot chocolate, bed, a movie, popcorn, and nobody to talk to me unless they're bringing me pillows.

I am no expert on hormones, but there are experts available to us, and it is supremely important that we as women honor ourselves and take the time to discover what is going on in our bodies and when. Hormones affect us emotionally, physically, and spiritually. For some of us the effect is painful and emotionally damaging. But we do not need to suffer by remaining alone in it. There is help available to us on many fronts. Talk to a friend, a pastor, a counselor, a doctor. See a naturopath, a gynecologist, a hormone specialist. And lean into God. Press in. The difficult days of each month can become a respite of hiding our hearts in our God, who always understands us and loves us endlessly. There is grace here. There is mercy here. For every one of us.

But let us begin here: do not curse yourself by cursing your body or your femininity. To be a woman is a glorious thing. Yes, we bear a suffering that men do not know. This is not a reason to envy them or to curse ourselves. (By the way, you curse yourself when you say things like, "I hate my body; I hate my period; I hate hormones; I wish I was a man.") Healing here begins with blessing:

> *I bless my body. I thank you, God, for making me a woman.*
> *I accept my body and my femininity as a gift. I bless these hor-*
> *mones inside me. I consecrate my feminine body to the Lord*

Jesus Christ; I consecrate my hormones to him. Jesus, come and
bring grace and healing here. Speak peace to the storm within
me just as you calmed the sea. Come and bless my femininity,
and teach me to understand how you have made me and how
to live with myself and the rhythms of my body.

Now, this was a brief glimpse at the internal setting of every woman's life. Time to turn our attention to the external landscape we all share. It might be more powerful than hormones, and I'll guarantee you that it's having a mighty impact on many an unaware woman.

the war around us

I recently read a story about a twelve-year-old girl in Ethiopia who had been abducted by men who planned to force her into marrying one of them. She'd been missing for a week when she was found. Terrified and bloody after having been severely beaten, the girl was being guarded by three lions that had come to her rescue and chased her captors away. Three man-eating lions that would normally attack people had miraculously saved her![4]

I love this story of another trinity coming to one in need. But after reading it, I learned that kidnapping and abusing girls in order to get them to marry is a common practice in Ethiopia. The United Nations estimates that more than 70 percent of marriages in Ethiopia come into being by abduction.

I'm not picking on Ethiopia here. Its history and current state of affairs mirror way too many other countries. The statistics on suffering in the world are mind numbing. But here is the story of *one* girl. I am amazed and grateful for this rescue and grieved for the millions of other girls who don't experience rescue themselves.

Most little girls at some point dream of living in a fairy tale. The big surprise when we grow up is not that the fairy tale was a myth but that it is far more dangerous than we thought. We do live in a fairy tale, but it often seems as if both the dragon and the wicked witch are winning. (Sometimes we feel that *we* are the dragon—that's the internal monthly battle, usually around week three.) But let me say with utmost seriousness, there is a battle going on around us every single moment of our waking and sleeping. The external landscape that we share is in the midst of a battle not only between good and evil but between life and death.

Things are not what they were meant to be. East of Eden, we have kept moving east and come all the way 'round, finding the garden utterly lost and cruelly unrecognizable. We were all born into *this* world. We came in gasping for air, and we are gasping still. It's a tough place to make a living, a hard place to make a life. Fire and ice. Beauty and terror. Pain and healing. Intertwined.

The good news is that Life wins out. Life has already won out. Love has won out. But the battlefield remains where we find ourselves, and the setting of the battle is a world that fiercely hates women. God loves women. Jesus loves women. The Enemy, the Devil, has women in his crosshairs.

Not a cheery thought but one necessary to face. Your life's journey runs through unfriendly terrain. You knew this already. The smoke from the heavenly engagement going on all around us affects our watery eyes and our labored breathing like smog. With mortars flying, aimed at our heart, we need to name it. So much of the sorrow in our lives finds its roots in misogyny.

the hatred of women

Misogyny: a hatred of women. From Greek misein *"to hate"* + gynē *"woman."*[5]

The Greek philosopher Aristotle lived three hundred years before Christ and had a huge effect on the world as we know it. He believed that women exist as natural deformations or imperfect males.[6] He was not alone in his belief, and that belief has had an effect. That's the world you were born into. Misogyny colors our world, and the colors have bled into your life. Recognizing it helps us understand our life and navigate through it.

Misogyny is the hatred of women and everything female. It was birthed at the fall of man and has found its home not only in men but in women, too. It manifests itself in many different ways—from jokes to pornography to sex trafficking to the self-contempt a woman feels for her own body. Why is plastic surgery now common practice? Anorexia, bulimia, and binging all find their roots in self-loathing, in misogyny. The history of our world is rampant with damage, oppression, diminishment, contempt, and fear *aimed* at women.

When Jesus came onto the scene he turned misogyny on its head. A rabbi at that time wouldn't speak to a woman in public, not even his own wife (this is still true for orthodox rabbis). Even today, an orthodox Jewish man is forbidden to touch or be touched by any woman who is not his wife or a close family relation. Jesus didn't abide by those rules. During his ministry Jesus engaged with women many times. He spoke to them. He touched them. He taught them. He esteemed them. He had women minister to him physically, touching him, washing his feet, anointing him with oil and with their tears. He had women disciples traveling with him, supporting him, learning from him, and "sitting at his feet." If we, the church, the body of Christ, had followed the example that Jesus had set instead of the traditions of men held captive to sin and the fall, we would have a much higher history here.

But misogyny got into the church. A long time ago. Many a Scripture-filled sermon has been preached throughout the centuries, advocating the suppression of women. We need to understand that the Bible records information and cultural practices that it does not *support*. The Bible describes in detail many acts of sin, but it does not endorse those acts. So it is with slavery—the Bible acknowledges it but does not endorse it. Yet slavery was supported from many pulpits in nineteenth-century America with sermons quoting Scripture. In the same way, Paul's words about women have too often been twisted to serve the oppression of women—far from his intention.

The church has been horrifically skewed regarding women. It has taught that women are the source of evil, that sex itself is evil. Some churches continue to teach that the fall of man came because of Eve's wickedness and that she and all women after her are temptresses. Churches have taught that women can't teach, women can't speak in church, women can't cut their hair. Women need to cover their bodies, their faces, their heads. They should stay quiet, stay separate from men, and really should just stay home. Women can't own property or vote or testify in court or travel alone. Women can't go to school because they simply aren't worth educating.

The good news is, it's changing. The truth also is that Christianity has done more to elevate the status of women than any other movement in history.

But in far too many cultures it is not changing at all. Yes, "we've come a long way, baby," but we've got a *long way to go*. Misogyny is fierce. It has come to us through people and governments and cultures and religions and nations. It comes through men. It comes through women. It can even come through little girls.

Think back to the playground. Little girls can be catty, cruel, and competitive. Generally speaking, boys slug each other and five minutes later have made up and moved on. Girls are laying strategies for revenge. They wound with sophistication and deadly words.

Women compete with each other for the attention of men. How many women have sacrificed their best friend on the altar of "boyfriend"? Many women are threatened by another woman's beauty, intelligence, and grace. We walk into a room and unconsciously size up all the other women in the room. We quickly judge where we fit in the hierarchy of attraction (worth) without even being aware that we have done it. That behavior finds its roots in misogyny. Remember, misogyny is hatred. Whether we are aware of it or not, when we hate women, we are hating ourselves, cooperating with the Enemy, and perpetuating grave damage. To hate, Jesus said, is to murder.

So of course misogyny can lead to physical acts of violence. From women. From men. In 2 Samuel we read:

> No sooner had Amnon raped her than he hated her—an immense hatred. The hatred that he felt for her was greater than the love he'd had for her. (2 Sam. 13:15 MSG)

Amnon, son of King David, fell in love with his beautiful half-sister Tamar and was frustrated "to the point of illness" that she was out of his reach. On the counsel of a friend, Amnon pretended to be bedridden with sickness and requested that Tamar be sent to care for him. Once Tamar was in his room, Amnon sent all the others away and asked her to come to bed with him. When Tamar refused, pleading with him to consider her humanity and his, Amnon raped her. After satisfying himself and devouring her beauty, Amnon's "love" immediately turned to hatred.

Sam Jolman, a counselor who blogs about men's issues, connects lust with misogyny:

> As Dan Allender says, "Lust is not about sex. It's about power." Lust is a man's attempt to dominate a woman. To strip her of her power. Rape is the obvious picture of this. Rape has nothing to do with sex. The pleasure in rape lies in the momentary experience of power. Notice how the savage brutality of war and genocide always involves murdering men and raping women. These are not lonely

soldiers looking for a little taste of love, but savages looking to slake their thirst for power.[7]

As is true for so many of you reading, my story includes sexual assault.
One instance occurred when I was twenty. A man followed me into a restaurant bathroom, locked the door behind him, and tried to force himself
on me. I fought him. He ended up pinning me between the commode and
the wall and pleasured himself. After climaxing, he released me and yelled,
"Look what you made me do! Look what you made me do!" Then he left.

Look what *you* made me do. He blamed me for his sin, his *hatred*. That
is not an uncommon slant of reality.

But let us be careful not to fall into blaming or hating men. May it
never be! Men are to be esteemed. And so are women. Masculinity is to
be relished. Celebrated. Honored. Welcomed. And so is femininity. The
sorrow men reaped at the fall includes their separation from God and their
separation from their *ezer*. God created Eve to be Adam's *ezer*, the Hebrew
word in Genesis 2:18 that means his lifesaver, his counterpart, the one
whom he literally cannot live and flourish without. God's intention was for
men and women to support and complete each other, to be one in purpose,
in mission, in love. But the fall came, and with it came division and sorrow
beyond telling. Though much of the sorrow in our lives flows from human
beings, people are not the enemy. Women are not the enemy. Men are not
the enemy. Satan is the Enemy.

the true cause

Two children are sold into the human sex trade every minute, with nearly
two million children forced into the worldwide sex trade each year.[8] Eighty
percent of those trafficking victims are women and girls. And human trafficking is not a problem only with other countries—it is rampant in the

United States as well. Human trafficking was expected to be the number-one crime in America in 2012. The United States is the number-one destination for sex tourism.[9]

Or how about this? Eighty percent of pornography that floods the world is rated as "hard-core" porn.[10] When most of us think of pornography, what comes to mind is "soft" porn. Hard-core pornography includes child pornography, sado-masochistic pornography, insanely beyond-wicked pornography. All aimed to destroy the hearts of every person coming near it.

The source of all this hatred and sorrow is not men, not the church, not even governments or systems of injustice. Scripture makes it very clear that the source of evil is the Evil One himself:

> For our struggle is not against flesh and blood, but against
> the rulers, against the authorities, against the powers of
> this dark world and against the spiritual forces of evil in
> the heavenly realms. (Eph. 6:12)

Evil is rampant. And it is far too easy to blame people, organizations, movements, the church, or political systems. But that will never change things because that is a naive understanding of the world. Jesus called Satan the prince of this world. Satan is the prince of darkness, whose sole aim is to steal, kill, and destroy life in all its forms, and he has power here. He has power here on earth, where and when the kingdom of God is not being enforced or advanced. He is the source of the hatred of women, the hatred you have endured. But let us remember: Jesus has won all victory through his crucifixion, resurrection, and ascension. All authority in heaven and on earth has been given back to him, where it rightly belongs. And then Jesus gave it to us.

I'll have more to say about this in a coming chapter. For now let us acknowledge two things:

There is great evil in the world, my sister, and much of it is directed at women.

The source of that evil is not men, or women, but Satan.

If you will accept this, you can not only make leaps forward in understanding your life, but you can find your way through the battle to the goodness God has for you and the goodness he wants to bring through you.

the way forward is love

Just as we cannot overcome our feminine bodies by hating them, we cannot overcome misogyny by hating women, or men. When we hate women, we hate ourselves. When we diminish the role of women, we diminish ourselves. When we are jealous, envious, slandering other women, we join the Enemy's assault on them. In doing those things we come into agreement with the Enemy of our hearts and of God by saying that what God has made is *not* good. It's time to stop doing that. The way to navigate the external battle begins with love. Not blaming, not finger-pointing, but love.

Yes, the roles that have been dominated in the past by the female persuasion are the roles that are less valued by our society. Providing the backbone of our world and paid ridiculously low salaries are teachers, nurses, caregivers, professional assistants, you name it. Their work is diminished. The role of mother has been minimized as well. "Do you work?" means "Do you have a real job that requires something of you, or do you just stay home and bake cookies all day?"

Puhlease.

But we do not overcome this subtle misogyny by trying to be men any more than we overcome our feminine bodies by trying to "unsex ourselves" as Lady Macbeth attempted. Let us begin by celebrating the role we play; let us champion these callings and celebrate them every way we can. The truth is that who we are as women, what we bring, and the role that is ours to play in the world, in the kingdom of God, and in the lives of men, women, and children are of immeasurable worth and power.

The kingdom of God will not advance as it needs to advance without women rising up and playing their role. The transformation and healing of a man requires the presence, strength, and mercy of a woman. Men will not become the men they are meant to be without godly women pouring into their lives. Women will not become who they are meant to be without the strength, encouragement, and wisdom of other women nurturing their lives. Yes, it's been hard. But that's because you are so vitally needed. Your valiant feminine heart is needed today in the lives of those you live with, work with, and love. The hour is late.

Women are image bearers of God. Women are coheirs with Christ. Women are valued, worthy, powerful, and needed. There is a reason the Enemy fears women and has poured his hatred onto our very existence. Let him be afraid, then. For "we are hard pressed on every side, but not crushed; perplexed, but not in despair; persecuted, but not abandoned; struck down, but not destroyed" (2 Cor. 4:8–9). We are more than conquerors through Christ who strengthens us, and we will not be overcome. God is our strength. Jesus is our defender. The Holy Spirit is our portion. And in the name of our God and Savior, we will choose to love him. We will choose to bow down in surrendered worship to our God. And by the power of Christ in us, we will choose to rise up and be women of God, bringing his kingdom in unyielding and merciful strength.

4

our mothers, ourselves: part 1

Mark volunteered at an after-school program, tutoring high school students in English. Sister Janet was the driving force behind all aspects of the program. Sister Janet found out that Mark played the cello well, so she asked him to play for a school assembly.

Mark was not gung ho on the idea. He told Sister Janet that assemblies featuring classical music do not go well; they can get ugly. Sister Janet replied that their boys would never behave in an ugly way. Their "boys," by the way, were young men ages fifteen to seventeen, incarcerated in the Los Angeles Juvenile Detention Center, awaiting trial for crimes ranging from armed robbery to murder.

And she wanted Mark to play the cello.

Sister Janet was a force to be reckoned with, so she convinced Mark. The day of the assembly came, and Mark was escorted by a guard to the side room adjacent to the stage and told to wait. While he was waiting, he could hear the blasting sound of hip-hop music and the young men going crazy with happiness. He ventured a peek out the door and saw that the star of the show was a scantily clad young woman, musically challenged, banging on a tambourine.

Mark closed the door and slumped in his chair. In walked Sister Janet. Mark exclaimed, "This was a huge mistake! Listen to them out there! They're going crazy, and all that for a girl in a bikini!"

"There's a girl in a bikini out there?" Sister Janet asked, intrigued.

"It might as well be a bikini!" Mark whined.

"Have a little faith," Sister Janet urged.

The time came for the hip-hop group to leave. The guard opened the door for Mark and motioned for him to come onto the stage. As he walked across the stage, Mark tripped over his cello, earning laughter and applause.

Not anxious to play, he regaled the audience with interesting (to him) and boring (to them) facts about the cello until he just couldn't put it off any longer. "I'd like to play 'The Swan' for you. It's a song that always reminds me of my mother."

Mark began to play. The concrete floors, the bare walls, and the high ceilings made the room as resonant as a shower stall. The music was beautiful. But then he began to hear another sound, the sound of restlessness. Movement. Shuffling. Oh great, he thought, they're bored already. Risking a glance, he saw that the noise he heard was snuffling. The young men were wiping their runny noses on their sleeves. Tears flowed down their faces. Mark continued to play "The Swan" better than he had ever played it. When he finished, it was to rousing applause.

"Now I'd like to play a saraband by Bach." Mark again played well. After the smattering of applause, one young man yelled out from the back, "Play the one about mothers again!"

Oh.

It was not so much the beauty of the music that had moved the inmates but rather the invocation of motherhood. Mark played the song two more times and received a standing ovation. The young men booed the guard when he came to escort Mark off the stage.[1]

Mother.

In *The Pastor's Wife*, Sabina Wurmbrand shared that at night, in prison, when all is quiet, one word is called out in the darkness most often. It is a plea and a prayer all in one: "Mother."

On battlefields when the fighting is done and soldiers lie wounded and dying, one word is universally called out: "Mother!"

I called it out. I was twelve years old, and my brother had finally allowed me to ride his minibike. He gave me instructions on all things save one: how to stop. Our driveway was long and steep, and the trees bordering it hid the road. I flew down the driveway, increasing in speed as I went, sped straight across the road, smashed into the curb, and flew over the minibike, breaking my fall on the neighbor's wooden fence.

"Mom!" I cried.

She came running. She came with Mr. Next-Door Neighbor, and the two of them helped me limp to my room to my bed. A short while later, my mom came in to check on me, and her words were, "You need to lose weight. You were really hard to carry because you are so heavy. It was embarrassing."

Mother.

It's a powerful word for a powerful woman who has made all kinds of impact on your life. Our mothers have blessed us and have wounded us. It's now time to pursue more of the healing Jesus has for us by turning our attention to our mother wound, which for some of us is the Mother of all Wounds. (Big breath. Keep breathing.)

the power of a mother

I was watching over my sons at the playground one afternoon when our oldest (only five at the time) began to move in a forbidden direction. In a flash this noise burst out of my mouth that sounded like a machine gun: "AH! AH! AH! AH!" I had never made that sound before. But my mother had. I looked around. Where had *that* come from? Aren't you shocked when your mother suddenly emerges—through *you*?

We say, "I'm becoming my mother!" And this is usually not spoken with glee. There is a tension between mothers and daughters that feels almost primal. Sometimes our differences alone can become a source of division. My mother didn't like the ocean and barely knew how to swim, and I am part fish. She got heat stroke if she was out in the sun for too long, and I love the sun. She dressed classically and conservatively, and I don't like button-down shirts. Collars give me hair rats. She preferred tennis shoes. I prefer flip-flops. She thought I should cut my hair. I still haven't.

Yet there are things about my mother that I so love. My mother loved to garden. I love to garden. She loved to bake. I love to bake. She decorated the house for holidays. I do that. She liked to entertain. I enjoy having people over. She sponsored a child forty-five years ago before most people knew the opportunity existed, and she brought orphans to our home to spend the day playing. I hope I'm like that. She was self-controlled and self-disciplined, and how come I didn't get more of that? Honestly, there are many, many ways I would *like* to become like my mother.

Lillian Hellman said, "My mother was dead for five years before I knew that I loved her very much."

Luckily for me—and thank you, Jesus—I figured it out before my mom passed away ten years ago.

It's easy to blame our mothers. Children will blame their moms when they are hurt (so will teenagers). I was walking down the stairs behind my son Sam when he was about four years old, and he knocked his hip on the stair rail. It made a big thump sound and I knew it had to hurt, but what he did next surprised me: he turned to me with a glare and growled, "Mom!" What? I didn't do it to him! Why is he blaming me?

We want to honor our mothers.

The command to honor your father and your mother is found several times in Scripture. It is the only command with a promise attached. "Honor your father and your mother, so that you may live long in the land the LORD your God is giving you" (Exod. 20:12). Your land may be land, or it may be a calling, a business, a relationship, a ministry. Your land is your territory, your domain.

Mothers teach, counsel, and guide. "Do not forsake your mother's teaching" (Prov. 1:8). Mothers comfort. "As a mother comforts her child, so will I comfort you" (Isa. 66:13). Mothers are a source of wisdom. The famous Proverbs 31 was written by King Lemuel as "an inspired utterance his mother taught him" (Prov. 31:1 TNIV). There is a reason Proverbs personifies wisdom as a woman. Lady Wisdom walks in grace and wisdom purchased over decades of choices to cultivate her heart by faith. Wisdom is earned. And a mother passes her wisdom, her way, her core beliefs onto her children. "I am reminded of your sincere faith, which first lived in your grandmother Lois and in your mother Eunice and, I am persuaded, now lives in you also" (2 Tim. 1:5).

Too often we have diminished our mothers, both who they are and what they've done. We want to respect the weighty role they have played in our lives.

We also need to be honest about our mothers—they have affected us far more than most of us realize. How could it be otherwise?

Women are made in the image of God. Remember, God said, "'Let us make mankind in our image....' In the image of God he created them; male and female he created them" (Gen. 1:26–27 NIV 2011). That means that our feminine hearts find their root in the heart of our Creator God. I am not questioning the gender of God or the fact that God is our heavenly Father. He most definitely, profoundly is. He is not our heavenly Parent. Father is masculine. But the Trinity—God the Father, God the Son, and God the Holy

Spirit—does not have a gender but is *the source of gender.* There is the father heart of God. There is also the *mother heart* of God. I put some words earlier to what a mother is meant to do: teach, guide, impart wisdom, comfort. Does that sound like any member of the Trinity to you? The Holy Spirit maybe?

You carry so much dignity simply because you are a woman. You are an image bearer of the living God. Priceless. Integral.

In order to increasingly become who we truly are, we need to increasingly pursue deeper healing with Jesus. So with that in mind and heart, I want to gently explore our mother wound, but you should know right off that I am not going to throw our mothers or ourselves under a bus. Not a one of us is a perfect mother, and none of us had one. God alone is perfect. I do not want to usher in guilt or shame or accusation or regret or resentment. No. In Jesus's name, no.

A great deal has been written on the impact a father has on his son or daughter. My husband and I have both talked about this ourselves in previous books (*Captivating, Wild at Heart, Fathered by God*). Every child enters the world with a core question, and the primary person they bring their heart's question to is their father. For men the question is, *Do I have what it takes? Am I the real deal?* For women it's, *Do you delight in me? Am I captivating?* But for both girls and boys, the deepest question is, *Do you love me?*

Because of the way God has created the universe, the father-child relationship is the deepest in our souls. The father bestows identity. *This is who you are. This is your true name.* How your father answered those questions for you helped shape you into the woman you are today. Your earthly father played and is still playing an enormously defining role in your life.

It can easily follow in our thinking that mother must play a secondary, incidental role. But why would we believe that what the father offers his children is of the utmost importance and what the mother offers her children is … ummmm … clean underwear and Easter baskets? Got a great father? Super. You're all set.

Oh, if only. No. The role of mother is profound, and the role *your* mother has played and continues to play in your life is utterly central to shaping the woman you are today.

Father bestows identity.

Mother bestows *self-worth*.

did your mother value you?

As a woman, your mother is your most potent role model. How she felt, what she thought, and what she believed had a direct effect on you.

What our mom felt about her body affected deeply how we feel about our bodies. What she believed also affected what we believe, including what we believe is possible in relationships: what men are like, what marriage can be like, how happy we can be. Our mom impacted what we think is possible in this life—what we can attain, achieve, and become. How high we set goals and dreams and even how we care for ourselves.

It's important to take a look at that. Her effect on us is not a life sentence on us, because Jesus has come for us and we have been adopted into a new family; we have a new bloodline. But all that our mothers believed was passed on to us. And we need to become aware of it. What did or does your mother believe? How did or does she treat herself and her needs?

Are you worth sacrificing for? Are you worth being inconvenienced for? Taking the time for? Loving? Do you have any worth? Your mother is the one who answered these questions in your heart. And not just her daughter's heart's questions but her son's, too.

Your mother's effect on you is profound. It is foundational, emotional, mental, physical, spiritual, and cellular. She played an enormously defining role in your life that began when you were in your mother's womb, continued on while you were an infant, and progressed through every stage of your life until this very moment.

A baby being formed in the womb knows much, feels much, even hears much. It's documented that a baby in the womb is *aware* and that at some deep level we actually remember what was happening in our world while we were in there. If while in the womb, a baby has a stressed, fearful, or angry mother, it has a direct effect on the developing baby. The mother's emotions transfer to the baby. The issues a mother struggles with transfer as well. For example, if a mom is substantially overweight while pregnant, chances increase exponentially that the child when grown will struggle with obesity as well. Actually, if the mom struggles with any kind of addiction, the potential increases dramatically that her child will as well.

I have battled with obesity for the better part of the past thirty years. My mother, however, was not overweight when pregnant with me, so I can't lay the blame for any obesity at her feet. Darn. She was, though, deeply overwhelmed and profoundly depressed. I was a baby whose arrival was a cause not for celebration but for weeping. My mother didn't know how in the world she could manage another child or even *survive.*

What happens in the womb sets the foundation for your life. When a mother is happy, secure, and hopeful, the blood flow to her uterus opens up and fully nourishes the fetus. When a mother is worried, anxious, or fearful, the blood vessels constrict, and the flow of blood to the fetus is constricted. The developing baby does not get enough. If that experience is predominant, the baby comes to believe in her core that she will not have enough; she is not secure, not safe, and not taken care of.[2]

Questions are being answered in her tiny heart: *Am I secure? Will there be enough for me? Enough food? Enough emotional nourishment? Am I wanted? Rejoiced over? Panicked over? Am I coming into a dangerous living environment or a safe one?*

A baby in the womb can hear voices. She will recognize her mother's voice upon birth. You see, a mother is a mother as soon as she conceives. All that is going on in her life during those nine months of gestation *matters*. It affects the child. It affected you.

While you were being formed in your mother's womb, think on it: Do you think you were satisfied? Did you get enough? Was your mother stressed, afraid? Worried? Did she smoke? Drink? Was she excited about being pregnant or terrified of it?

Since your mom was a human being, there were definitely times when she was stressed by the prospect of your arrival. And once their baby arrives, most mothers have moments or months of feeling pretty overwhelmed. You give birth to a baby, and they just send you home with it.

As a first-time mother, I got hit pretty hard with postpartum depression, and for the life of me I couldn't understand how any child had ever survived. I was overwhelmed by the responsibility, the prospect of caring for and raising a child. Those same feelings accompany a mother who has adopted her child as well. And we can safely assume that adopted babies had birth mothers who were at times filled with anxiety too. If you were adopted, you had a birth mother who loved you profoundly and unselfishly enough to relinquish your precious self to a family she knew could offer you what she could not. You yourself may have made that incredibly difficult and utterly loving choice. God bless you for that. God knows what that has been like.

mother as nurturer

The first primary role of mother is nurturing, the giving of care that engenders life. It involves meeting the vast range of physical, emotional, social, and spiritual needs a child has in order to grow and develop healthily. A child needs food, shelter, clothing, medicine, care, comfort, and touch.

Once born, the gift of mothering hormones aids a new mother, helping her meet the needs of her *very needy* baby. To answer his or her cry for food, for comfort, to be held, to be changed, to be valued. Again. And again. And again. And the infant is taking note. This is where we learn: *Do my needs matter? Am I valuable? Is the world safe? Will I be taken care of? Protected? Nurtured? When I need it? Or when it's more convenient? Or never?*

Infants given up for adoption in too many developing countries spend hours and days and months alone in their cribs, being held or merely touched just once or twice a day as necessary. A child who is not held enough develops into an adult with a myriad of emotional difficulties, just as an inadequate diet manifests as health problems later in life. The damage to the human soul treated with such callous disregard is cataclysmic. But we don't have to go far away to find damage. We can go next door. Or back to our own childhood.

The first two years of a person's life are *the* years where the sense of self and self-worth is formed. And who is primarily responsible for that setting? Mom. Even if she is a full-time out-of-the-home working mother who must return to her position when her infant is just two weeks old, it is not the caregiver who is forming her child's heart. It is the mom.

We do not live in a perfect world. I am a mother myself who has failed my children in innumerable ways. So in talking about our mothers, I'm not looking to cast blame. We are searching for understanding and *healing*. You too may be a mother, and I am aware of the tension between looking back at our own childhoods and looking at our children's childhoods. We can easily become afraid that we've ruined them forever. You haven't, dear one. Yes, we've failed. Even the best of mothers fails her children. No one escapes the need for healing. No one escapes the need for God. We need him. So do our children.

For now, we want to stay present to *our* stories and the effect our mothers had on *our* lives. Let us venture back with God into our days—even those beyond our reckoning—so that we might receive God's healing. We need to do that before we focus on how we are mothering our children, and where God is calling us to change.

Were *you* satisfied? Once you were born, did you get enough? Food. Comfort. Safety. Love. Touch. Eye contact. Babies need their mother. They know her voice, her scent, her face. Infants respond exponentially more to a woman's face and voice than to a man's.

Were you satisfied *as a child*? Were your basic needs for food, safety, and good touch met? Did you receive the attention you needed? Was the delight bestowed on you that you were meant to have? Were you celebrated simply because you existed as yourself? Not getting enough feels the same as rejection. Not having your basic needs satisfied creates a deep sense of being unworthy and not enough, that something is wrong with you.

My mother smoked and drank while carrying me, back in the day when they all thought that was fine. (I know—can you believe it?) She was overwhelmed by her pregnancy with me. She was angry, scared, and, in her own words, "devastated" by my existence. I did not get enough while in the womb. There was added fear because I was a high-risk pregnancy. My mother had almost bled to death giving birth to my two previous siblings and having a baby was dangerous for her. They scheduled a C-section to deliver me, and there were risks involved.

When I was born, it was into a family with an absent father and a mother who told my sisters that when they woke up, she would be gone. They would wake up and run into her bedroom to see if she was still there. My mother could not satisfy me. She did not have enough for me. Food. Time. Touch. Love. Attention. Care. Delight. Play.

Phillip Moffit of the Life Balance Institute wrote,

> If you did not receive sufficient nurturing in childhood, as an adult you may feel an insatiable need, an inability to take joy in others, or a lack of self-worth despite your competency and confidence.[3]

Does that sound familiar to anyone besides me?

By contrast, the psalmist says,

> But I have calmed and quieted my soul,
> like a weaned child with its mother;
> like a weaned child is my soul within me. (Ps. 131:2 ESV)

There is hope for us. There is healing. Nothing is out of reach for Jesus. "Weaned" means satisfied. *I am satisfied. I have had enough. All is well.* A weaned child is a satisfied child. Full. Content. Has enough. We can know that. We can.

God has used the healing of my mother wound to unlock the unsatisfied and starving places deep within me. It has been one of the final keys to free me from an ungodly attachment to food. I began to pray for Jesus to come into the unsatisfied places of my heart and to proclaim the truth that in Christ I have all I need. I began to agree with God that my soul is satisfied in him. I don't have to fear never getting enough anymore. I don't have to arrange for my own provision, protection, or comfort. I already have more than enough, and I always will. When I began praying that, something mysterious happened. (We'll get more into that in a moment.)

We all have a deep soul hunger, and the only satisfaction we will find for that is in the presence of God. The unseen. The eternal. The uncreated one. Who says *he will satisfy your desires with every good thing*. Ultimately, with himself.

mother as protector

Another crucial role that a mother is meant to play is that of protector. This is instinctive. A child needs to be protected from physical, sexual, and emotional abuse, and from the threat of all three.

This is where the Mother Bear comes in. The "you don't mess with my child" thing. I was at the playground once with friends, all of whom were mothers of young children. We were watching our children play from a distance while we talked. The younger ones were toddling around in the sand, while the older ones were swinging. Suddenly one of the little ones walked directly in front of the swing as his brother was heading back and up, up, up. The toddler had set himself up like a bowling pin in the direct line of the swing. He was going to be kicked hard and hurt badly.

His mother flashed like a gazelle. She ran through the sand, grabbed her child, leaped out of the way, and swoosh, down came the swing. It was amazing. Really! We all cheered.

A mother protects. Or she is meant to. She is supposed to know what is going on in her child's life. To notice. To be aware. And to intervene.

Did your mother notice? Did she intervene?

My mother may have noticed, but she did not intervene. She saw, but she turned her face away. Whether it was too difficult for her in the moment because of the enormity of the sorrow in her own life, or because she simply did not have the tools or the capacity to intervene, she did not. How I wish she had.

It was prom night. Rain thwarted our plans to go to the beach after the dance, so we went back to my house. My mother would have been asleep for a long while. My brother's bedroom was at the far end of the house, attached to the kitchen. Private. Separate. We quietly snuck into his bedroom and closed the door. In an effort to win this boy's heart, I offered my body. Before we were intimate, but lying on the bed in heated desire, there was a noise at the door. My mother was on the other side. We froze. We didn't move again until we heard her walk away. And then we went back at it.

The course of my life might have been dramatically different had my mother possessed the courage to knock on the door and walk in. *Might* have been. But she didn't. Following countless other times of her inability to speak into or intervene in my life, this one event, all the events really, had a profound and damaging effect.

Did your mother honor you with the self-worth you deserved by intervening on your behalf, regardless of how difficult or uncomfortable it may have been for her?

Mothers bestow our self-worth, and they have the ability to withhold it. Intentionally, but more often unintentionally. A mother cannot pass on what she does not possess. And neither can we. Mothers have the ability to withhold acceptance, value, love. Our mothers failed us when, without meaning to, they passed on to us low self-esteem. Or based our self-worth on anything other than the fact that we exist.

God does not do that.

Our worth is not based on what we do, which life path we choose, or what we believe. Our worth is inherent in the fact that we are image bearers of the living God. Our worth is based on the fact that we are alive. We are human beings. Our worth is immeasurable.

Our worth as a woman does not come to us when we believe in Jesus Christ as our Savior. It comes in our creation.

If we were not of great worth, then the blood of goats and lambs, oxen and bulls, would have been enough to purchase humanity out of captivity. Back in the garden of Eden, you remember, the human race went into captivity, and the price to buy us back was so high that no ransom note was even sent. But God knew and pursued us. He intervened.

God paid the ultimate necessary ransom to buy us out of the captivity of sin and the Devil. We are all hostages of such value that it took the blood of God himself to pay our price. You have a worth beyond counting. Right now.

mother as preparer

The third critical role a mother is meant to play is to prepare her child, encouraging independence and teaching self-confidence. Mom is meant to prepare her child to become her equal and even to surpass her. The ability to do this well flows from the mother's own self-confidence. Her self-perception cannot be tied to how her child is doing. (No one said this was going to be easy.) Encouraging self-reliance and providing education, discipline, and creative opportunities help to prepare her child to live her own life.

A mother is supposed to be a student of her child's heart. *What do you love? What do you like? It matters! You matter!* Her interests are met with enthusiasm. The child is encouraged to *try.* She can fail and still be fully accepted. In fact, failing is simply seen as evidence that she is trying! A mother empowers her child by speaking the truth—speaking acceptance and love into her child's life.

Okay. Pause. You may be getting overwhelmed now. Breathe. Come for us, Jesus.

As a child, were you accepted? Seen? Celebrated? Were you encouraged to pursue your interests? To try?

And what about as a teenager and a young woman? You see, you still need all of it—food, safety, comfort, love, touch, eye contact. We function best when we receive at least two extended hugs a day, and I mean long hugs. Not this A-frame business. Did you receive attention and delight? Do you remember receiving the encouragement to be you? To become your unique self? Were you welcomed into the realm of womanhood? Were you initiated into the feminine world with approval and a sense of belonging?

Do you even have any idea what I'm talking about?

Okay, how do you feel about your period? Is it "the curse," a hassle, and a major drag? What are some words you would use to describe it? Wonder? Amazement? The gift of being a woman and possessing the ability to carry and nourish life? What was your first period like? Who taught you how to use feminine products or how to shave your legs? How did you learn how to wash your face or care for your body, your skin, your hair? Were you blessed for being feminine or shamed for it?

How did your mother feel about her body? How did she feel about her period? More importantly, how did she feel about being a woman?

Do you begin to see now what I meant when I said that your mother has played a critical role in shaping you into the woman you are today? Without even thinking about it, your mother passed all that down to you and into you before you took your first breath.

pause

Our mother wounds are so important to our lives now and our futures before us that it is going to take two chapters to get where we need to be. But I have to pause for a moment and say, sister, hear me now: there is healing; there is hope. Whatever your mother's impact upon you, it is not a sentence on your life. What *you* believe, what *you* choose now is your path and your future. You are a woman! You are an amazing powerful image bearer of the living God. You are the beloved of Jesus Christ. To be able to embrace our womanhood and become who we are meant to be and offer what we were born to offer will require all of us to receive some healing here. We will pray through these issues together at the end of the next chapter.

5

our mothers, ourselves: part 2

We've talked about three of the four vital roles a mother plays in her children's lives: nurturer, protector, and preparer. Remember now—we are exploring this not in order to critique our own mothering at this time, but in order to understand why we have become the women we are, and more importantly to find those changes we have longed for over the years. Before we move on, I'd like to say a bit more about mother as Preparer, especially when it comes to preparing her daughter for womanhood. Very few of us had the kind of preparation God intended us to have so that we might grow up into confident, resilient, loving women. So let me offer a picture here through what one of my friends offered her daughter.

welcoming Kacey into womanhood

Becky is a woman I have come to love and respect. When her daughter Kacey began to mature, Becky and her husband, Jim, started to prepare Kacey for all that was coming with intention. I'll let Becky tell the story in her own words:[1]

We used the American Girls book entitled *The Care and Keeping of You* to begin the dialogue of what she could expect. We talked about her beauty in God's eyes, that she is a masterpiece created by our God. We went to a fun restaurant where we ordered special drinks in a mug, but I brought a Styrofoam cup, too. We talked about how she is not "throw away" like Styrofoam, or serviceable like a mug; then I pulled out fine china and said she is like "fine china," priceless, hand painted, and carefully cared for. We shopped for her first bras and made that very special!

On the next outing, we talked about what she likes about her body and what she doesn't … that was great dialogue. One week we had pedicures and talked about the source of true beauty, using principles from *Captivating* to give her Jesus's true perspective. Lastly, we talked about beginning her monthly cycle, and I gave her a little bag with all the things she would need, just in case. The actual day she began her monthly cycle, we made into a very special event with a date out to ice cream.

I just have to pause for a moment and say I know, I know—let the tears come. For all that you wished you had and did not receive. I share Kacey's story not only to help you know what you were meant to have, but also to awaken your heart to the healing Jesus longs for you.

Throughout these couple of years, Jim began to date Kacey; the big event every year was taking her to the Daddy-Daughter dance held here locally. This past spring, at age fourteen, was the last dance they got to attend, and how perfect to have had her "calling forth" ceremony the same year, in this year of transition. Jim made this last dance very special by taking her shopping himself to find the "perfect" dress and accessories.

the calling forth ceremony

We prayed about what we were going to do for her Calling Forth ceremony. First of all, we kept it a complete surprise and also included family and friends who have played a key role in Kacey's life. Also, Jim had taken her shopping again one night, getting her a new dress (white) but not saying what it was for. As the evening began and after dedicating it to God in prayer, we told Kacey we were calling her out to be who *God said* she is.

Several weeks before this ceremony, Jim and I had asked her to write a paper, with no parameters, about what it means to be a Christian woman. We had her read to everyone what she had written; I believe this gave her ownership in all we were doing in her life.

Next, we showed the scene from the *Fellowship of the Ring* where Arwen rides with Frodo to the river. With her love of horses and her striking resemblance to Arwen, it really impacted Kacey's heart. Then our two boys, ages nine and seventeen, brought in Arwen's sword. Each of the boys spoke over Kacey and then handed me the sword. After them, I spoke over her life and what I see in her, and called her out as Arwen, as a warrior princess. We then passed the sword around, allowing each person to speak from their heart over Kacey's life. Lastly, the sword came to her dad, who then, after speaking, presented her with the sword.

We then explained that "Butterfly Kisses" was the song we played when she was dedicated to God as an infant, and began to play that song; about halfway through Jim asked her to dance. There was not a dry eye in the room. Then Jim took her on his lap and spoke about keeping herself pure; he pulled out a "promise ring" we had found especially for this evening. It has her birthstone in the middle, being supported or held up by my birthstone and Jim's. Inside the band of the ring it says "forever my daughter."

Then all gathered around Kacey, laying hands on her and anointing her for this next part of her life and sealing in her heart all that had been spoken. Some very dear friends presented her with a charm bracelet, where they each picked out a charm to give Kacey. The bracelet is incredibly meaningful to her. Throughout the whole evening a friend wrote down what each person said in a beautiful keepsake journal. Kacey goes back and reads it all the time and has added to it.

We have not done this parenting thing perfectly, but I believe that God has led us to give Kacey the tools, the affirmation of who she is in him, and the encouragement to live differently in a time that can be very hard for a teenage young woman. Just the other night Jim and I sat and held her together and prayed over her, building on all that we did in the Calling Forth ceremony.

I share this not because Becky and Jim did it all right, nor to suggest that this is *the* only model to follow. I share this because it is a beautiful picture of the love and intentionality *you* were meant to experience, the preparation you were supposed to receive as a young woman. *Come for us, Jesus. Come where we did not know any such thing. Come for our hearts.* We are going to pray a healing prayer at the end of this chapter, but let me first cover the fourth primary role a mother plays.

mother as initiator

We raise our children to leave us. It is perhaps the hardest and most beautiful truth of motherhood.

I dropped my sons Sam and Blaine off at the airport yesterday after far too short of a Thanksgiving break. Though we've said our good-byes curbside before, it remains painful. It is one of the sorrows of being a mother that we raise our children to leave us. And leave us is exactly what they need to do. Difficult as it is, mothers are supposed to bless and even celebrate their daughters and sons leaving home and moving into the next stage of their lives.

This involves separating from our children, cutting the apron strings and the invisible umbilical cord and letting them go—trusting they have the capacity to live their lives without our constant involvement. It involves providing, particularly in the teenage years and early adulthood, the sense that the mother understands her daughter *has the right* to become the full expression of her own unique self. And she blesses and encourages that. We need to have been let go of, and when the time comes, to let go of our own children as well. It is probably the hardest thing for a mother to do.

Some call this initiation. Full initiation into womanhood. When it does not occur, there is a sense of guilt in the adult child. The grown daughter feels responsible for the happiness and well-being of her mother. Often the mother, unable to let go, encourages this. Guilt is a weapon used by many a mother to manipulate her adult child. For a mother to be effective in providing initiation, she must have somehow received it herself.

How did your mother do with this most difficult of tasks?

The Disney movie *Tangled* presents a picture of a mother who is not blessing her daughter's life or letting her separate. The wicked woman (who is not actually her mother but pretending to be) uses fear to manipulate her daughter in order to keep what she wants: control over her daughter's life. She is a mother figure who refuses to let go. Though the film is fictional, the themes portrayed are many women's reality.

I have a dear friend whose mother has placed enormous demands on her life. Janie's mother has a massive spirit of entitlement and wields the weapon of guilt with skill. She acts as if she holds the keys to the front door of her grown daughter's home, not to mention Janie's life and heart, and that she has the right to walk into any of those realms at any moment she wishes. They talk on the phone at least once a day but usually more. My friend wants to honor her mother as God wants her to do but has wrongly believed that means her mother *does* have a right to her life. Her mother has held Janie hostage by fear and intimidation, and my friend has allowed her mother to continue to control her in countless ways. Her fear of being reproached by her mother, which she can't avoid, has led her to make choices that have compromised her own children's well-being and her relationship with her husband. Janie has not followed the biblical mandate to leave and cleave. She has put her relationship with her mother above her relationship with her husband (to her mother's delight). My precious friend sees it now and sorrows over it. But her mother is not going to change. It will be up to Janie to enforce the rightful boundaries over and around her life. (More on this in a coming chapter.)

Mothers do not have a right to their adult children's lives. They don't have the right to their children's emotional lives. Mothers need to be *invited in*. But first, mothers have to let go.

There is a scene near the end of the book and movie *The Help* that I love. Skeeter's mother—who has made all the classic mistakes of withholding her approval of her daughter, wanting her daughter to be just like her and to live the same kind of life that she herself has lived—finally and fully *blesses* her daughter. Perhaps for the first time, Momma has begun to see the woman her daughter has become and speaks life to her: "I have never been more proud of you." Looking straight into her daughter's eyes, her love, recognition, and release free Skeeter to continue on her own journey. It is beautiful.

> *Mothering well is a prayerful art.*
>
> —Lori McConnell, *Restoring Hope in a Woman's Heart*

healing

In her DVD *Mother-Daughter Wisdom*, Christiane Northrup described what we receive from our mothers as being similar to being dealt a hand of cards. What we received is formative and foundational, but this "hand" is *not* our destiny. If you didn't get dealt a great hand, say, or your cards are torn or bloody, folded or lousy or even missing, this is where the healing presence of Jesus Christ can come in and wash your cards clean. He gives you the cards he intended for you to have. He restores. He has established our destiny, which is to have him *formed in* us. He is our inheritance, and we must bring him our hearts, our wounds, all that we were meant to have as girls growing up. We bring him the hand we were dealt and ask for his healing. His name is Faithful and True. He is the same yesterday, today, and forever. He wants to heal us! Jesus is the one who has the right to speak into our lives with authority and power. He has the power to bless who we are and who we are becoming. We need to hear from him.

In order to receive the healing that God has for us regarding our mother wounds, we need to know what we need healing *from* and *for*. Specifically. We need to remember what happened in the story of our lives and invite the healing presence of Jesus there. For healing to come, we actually have to go back and remember and even access the emotion of the wound; Jesus helps us to do that.

The power of the memory to make the past present to us is extraordinary. The reason for this is that Jesus, the Infinite One who is outside time and to whom all times are present, enters into what for us is a past occurrence.
—Leanne Payne, *Crisis in Masculinity*

The events themselves do not change, but in the light of Jesus's love and presence, we are enabled to view and experience them differently. The sting of death is removed, the pain of the memory is released to Jesus, and healing comes. God will actually reframe our history and memories to us as he heals us. As God nurtures, protects, prepares, and initiates us, he restores us to the truth of who we are and the reality of the life we are living and meant to live. *We can be satisfied.* We *are* loved, wanted, seen, delighted in, provided for, cherished, chosen, known, and planned on. We are set apart, believed in, invited, valued, of immeasurable worth, and blessed.

Now it's time to pray. It would be helpful if you could get someplace quiet and private where you won't be interrupted for a bit. If you can't now, then wait until you can. Let's invite Jesus to come and reveal to us where he would love to bring us more healing.

But first there are some words that we may need to hear from our own mom that she may never be able to speak. It may be beyond her emotional or spiritual capacity, or she may have already died. Either way, I want to say to you, on *your mother's behalf:*

Sweetheart, I am so sorry. I am so sorry for having failed you in every way I have. I need your forgiveness. Please forgive me. Let God love you in the places that I didn't or couldn't as I should have. Forgive me. You deserved more.

Now to prayer. Take your time through this.

Holy Trinity, I invoke your healing presence now. Come and meet me here and now. I sanctify my memories and my imagination to you, God. I ask you to come and to reveal where I need healing, Jesus, and I ask you to heal me.

Where do you want to come, God? Where do I need you to come? Is it while I was in the womb? Is it as a child, a little girl, a young woman? Is it to every stage of my life?

Come, Jesus. I ask you to come for me and to heal me in the deep places and unseen realms of my heart. I need you. Come with your light and your love, come with your tender, strong, and merciful Presence and fill me here.

In the Name of Jesus, I bless my conception. God, you planned on me before the earth was made. I bless my development in my mother's womb. God, you were there. Come now beyond the bounds of time and minister to me, your precious one, as I was being formed in my inmost being, and speak your love and delight over me. I confess to you, God, and proclaim the truth that I have all I need. I am fully satisfied in you, Jesus, and I always will be. I am wanted, delighted in, and of immeasurable worth. You planned on me. You wanted me, and you still want me. Like a weaned child within me, my soul is satisfied in you, God.

I break off any and all curses assigned to me, including all judgments against me passed on from my generational line. I am adopted into your family. The very blood of Jesus has purchased me, and I belong to you forever as your daughter. I claim this right here, in the womb.

Together with you, Jesus, I bless my delivery. Come into that time and space, dear Jesus. Come into any and

all trauma or fear that I may have experienced in that.
I break off all assignments of fear or death that may have
entered in through a traumatic birth in the Name of Jesus
Christ.

   Jesus, my healer, come into my need for nurture; come
into the places that needed nurture from my mother. Show
me where healing is needed here.

As you linger through this prayer, Jesus will show you memories and events and bring back feelings that you had. Were you satisfied as a child? Were your basic needs—for food, safety, and healthy touch—met? Did you receive the attention you needed? Was the delight bestowed on you that you were meant to have? Were you celebrated simply because you existed as yourself? Linger, and invite Jesus here. As he reveals things to you, invite him in, ask him to heal. Is forgiveness needed here? Forgive. Are tears needed here? Allow those tears to come, but invite Jesus into those tears as you do. Ask his healing. Ask him to nurture you in this very place. Linger, and then continue with the prayer.

   Jesus, my healer, come into my need for protection; come into
the places that needed protection offered to me by my mother.
Show me where healing is needed here.

   A mother protects. She is supposed to know what is going on in her child's life. To notice. To be aware. To intervene. Did your mother notice? Did she intervene? Invite Jesus here.

   Jesus, my healer, come into my need for preparation; come
into the places that needed preparation from my mother.
Show me where healing is needed here.

A mother encourages her daughter toward independence and self-confidence. As a child were you accepted? Were you seen? Celebrated? Were you encouraged to pursue your interests? To try? Did you receive attention and delight? Do you remember receiving the encouragement to be you? To become your unique self? Were you welcomed into the realm of womanhood? Were you initiated into the feminine world with approval and a sense of belonging? Invite Jesus here.

> *Finally, Father God, in this moment I also repent of any and all hatred of women that has taken root in my heart. Hatred of women is hatred of myself and not from you. I choose to love women, and I embrace my own womanhood. I thank you that I am a woman! I bless my femininity! I thank you for my life, and I choose life. I give my life fully to you now, Jesus, and I invite you to have your way in me. I love you, Jesus. Thank you for coming for me; keep coming for me. I pray all of this in your glorious and beautiful Name, Jesus Christ. Amen.*

Okay. That was good. It really was. Whether you felt anything or not. It was good. Dear hearts, we *can* be satisfied. God put us in a world where we have him and we have one another. A woman once told me that there are all kinds of ways God brings daughters into our lives, and I have found that to be true. Well, it is also true that there are all kinds of ways God brings us mothers, too. Spiritual mothers. Friends. Counselors. Christ himself. Let God continue to mother you, to heal you. Stay with this. Continue to pray and press in toward the more that God has for you.

And know that, whether she ever conveyed it to you or not, you were a *gift* to your mother's heart of the grandest design. Every mother learns more from her children than she ever teaches them.

a lullaby of delight

John and I were visiting friends in Tucson recently, escaping the freezing temperatures of a Colorado winter for a brief respite to the warmth of the sun and the warmth of a welcome. After a restful day exploring the wonder of the desert, we gathered together for evening prayer. A phrase of one friend's prayer caught my imagination: "Father, sing your lullaby of delight over us."

As many mothers do, I used to make up songs for my children, singing lullabies softly to coax my young sons to sleep. Never remembering the correct words, I made them up as I went along, inserting their names often. I loved it. Turns out, they loved it too.

As I laid me down to sleep that night in Tucson, I asked God what his lullaby of delight over me sounded like. My mind immediately flashed to holy moments from earlier in the day: sitting alone in the shade, listening to the wind blow through the leaves of the eucalyptus trees towering above me, the sound like water, like the movement of life. I remembered the sound of the red-tailed hawks crying and calling to each other as they circled above their nearby nest. The song of quails and mourning doves and birds I didn't recognize added their melodies—a living symphony. Then all was quiet again save for the movement of leaves as another rolling breeze sang its way through the swaying trees.

A holy song. A lullaby of delight. Sung over me. Singing over you.

6

from accepting to embracing

Since love grows within you, so beauty grows. For love is the beauty of the soul.
—St. Augustine

"Do you love your hips?"

The question threw me. Why in the name of all that is holy would I love my hips? The woman standing in front of me at the conference where I had just spoken was waiting for my answer. She repeated herself. "Do you love your hips? 'Cuz Jesus is not gonna heal you till you love your hips!"

Oy. Of all the things not to love about myself, I hadn't given much thought to my hips, but thinking of them in that moment, I could definitely say no, I did not love my hips.

The woman was telling me the truth. She was saying, *God wants you to love and enjoy everything about yourself right now and embrace the truth that you are a beautiful woman regardless of your measurements.* Until we can do that, we will not be moving forward. Or downward, as the case may be.

It's a difficult thing to stand in front of a mirror naked and tell yourself how marvelous your body is. It is contrary to every broken thing in a woman's soul and in this broken world. But I began to do it. Not so God would change my body, f-i-n-a-l-l-y. But so that I could begin to align the way I see myself with the way he does.

I began one evening in the bathtub by thanking God for my legs. I told myself I had fabulous legs. "I haven't been so kind to you, legs, but we've been through a lot together and you've brought me far. Thank you, legs. You're awesome."

And on like that. It became a practice. I stumbled a bit when I came to my arms. I still struggle with the arms. But okay, I'm going to do it right now. "Thank you, God, for these amazing arms. They work and lift things and hold people and open jars and steer wheels and pick up all kinds of things. Wow. I'm sorry for neglecting you, arms. You really are something else."

beautiful now

One wonderful summer day last year, I was driving to Denver, rendezvousing with my husband at the wedding of some dear friends' son. I was wearing a pretty dress that I particularly loved. Wanting to look extra nice, underneath the dress I was wearing a modern-day girdle, a suck-you-in-all-over-so-you-can't-breathe-but-your-torso-will-be-smooth torture device.

In my own mother's day, and in many days before her, the device was a lace-up girdle. My mother wore one regularly. Most women of her generation did, just as so many women of our generation wear the newfangled version. My mom once told me the story of her grandmother's sister immigrating to the United States from Germany. She was coming over from Europe on a ship (of course), and wanting to look her best, she wore her corset. She wore her corset the entire two weeks. She wore her corset as cinched as she could get it. She wore her corset so cinched that it prevented her from being able to go to the bathroom, and by the end of the journey to the New World, she was dead. Because of her corset. True story. Oh sister, what price beauty?

Honestly, how many women have died in the quest to attain some just-out-of-reach level of beauty? It is a tragically high number.

So I was driving to Denver, wearing the hateful undergarment, when it became so painful I could barely breathe. It was driving into my ribs. I guess it's made for wearing while you are standing up, not sitting down for an hour behind a wheel. Thankfully, I was able to hoist my skirt up and get a hand underneath and pull the girdle thingy away from my body. But seriously, it took all my strength. I made a fist and let it press against that. Driving with one hand, at least I could breathe. But I needed to keep switching hands every few minutes because the thing was so unbelievably strong and tight.

And by the way, it was a size larger than I was currently wearing. So it's not that I had on the wrong size. It's that the things are supposed to strangle your body into a size or two smaller. Seriously now, why do we feel the need to do this to ourselves? What is so horrific about bumps? Please tell me. We are killing ourselves figuratively and literally to fit into the world's definition of what we are supposed to be.

My mother used to say, "Beauty before pain!"—meaning, being beautiful is more important than not feeling terrible. High heels with our toes pinched into the pointy tip. Spanx. Waxing. Trimming. Plucking. P-a-y-i-n-g.

One of the assignments my mother gave me as the youngest daughter in my family was to pluck the coarse black hairs protruding from her chin whenever she was no longer able to see them or care. She made me promise not to leave her to this indignity. She was a nurse who often tended older women, and she grieved for those whose personal grooming was ignored. My mom was well acquainted with those pesky little black hairs. She had a magnifying mirror in which she would look to peruse and destroy any interlopers. Pluck! Pluck! Pluck!

At about the age of thirty, I made the mistake of looking at myself in her well-lit magnifying mirror. WHAAAAT? Oh my gosh! Why did no one tell me I had a beard? Where are the tweezers? I was horrified. Are you kidding me? What was unseen to the mere human eye, or just by looking in a regular mirror—even up close—was magnified to werewolf proportions in my mother's mirror.

Pluck. Pluck. Pluck.

When my mother died, I got her mirror. I was hooked. Only some women know the satisfaction of a victorious plucking episode. When her mirror finally broke, I bought myself a new one. A bigger one. A better lit one. I encouraged my husband to look into it once and use it to pluck those nose hairs that seem to multiply as one gets older, and when he looked, he screamed. "Good grief! What? I'm a Wookie!" (A Wookie is a very tall creature covered completely with hair, found in the Star Wars movies. Chewbacca, Han Solo's trusted friend, is a Wookie. My husband, John, is not a Wookie. Except when looking in a very intense magnifying mirror.)

My husband had the good sense to know that the magnifying mirror wasn't reality. It isn't what anyone else sees. He refuses to look in it ever again, and he is urging me to throw the thing away. I have told him that throwing it away is in my future. But I'm not ready yet.

Maybe I'll be ready when I've attained a hair-free status. Or better, maybe I'll throw it away when my soul more fully embraces the truth of what God says about me. God has been inviting me to throw the magnifying mirror away and be free, free from gazing at my multiple imperfections in my face and in my soul and instead to believe the reflection he is showing me. Honestly, the only reflection that really matters is the reflection we see in his loving and joyous eyes. What does he see? What does he say? He says we are beautiful *now*.

> How beautiful you are, my darling!
>> Oh, how beautiful!
>> Your eyes behind your veil are doves. (Song 4:1)

Jesus is inviting us to relax into the beauty he has bestowed upon us and cease striving to attain a level of smooth perfection that looks wonderful on a doll or on a magazine cover but is not attainable in the living, breathing realm of humanity. God does not tell us that the goal is perfection. Perfection in any vital area of our life is not going to happen. There, I said it. Now, we can improve. We can grow. We can become more loving, more grace filled, more merciful. We are no longer bound to sin, slaves to its din of temptation. We are still going to sin. But we don't *have* to. The secret is Jesus.

Our hope doesn't rest on our finally getting it together. Our hope rests in Jesus. Jesus in us. It's Christ in us, the hope of glory. Paul says, "To them God has chosen to make known among the Gentiles the glorious riches of this mystery, which is Christ in you, the hope of glory" (Col. 1:27). We won't be perfect on this side of heaven. But Jesus is perfect. Always. We are becoming more holy and true. Jesus already is. His name isn't "Becoming." It is "I Am." Perfection isn't the goal. Jesus is.

God help me, one day soon I am going to break that mirror.

In the Song of Songs, God says,

> Let me hear your voice;
> for your voice is sweet,
>> and your face is lovely. (Song 2:14)

Lovely. Now isn't that a good word? The more I believe God, the lovelier I actually become. I rest in it. Oh, to not be a grasping, clutching, striving, unsatisfiable woman. God says I am, you are, lovely. Right at this very moment. Really. Breathe that in!

Every woman has a beauty unique unto herself. I have seen beauty in virtually every woman I have ever met regardless of skin type, body shape, hair color, teeth whiteness, or number on the scale. Every woman is beautiful. You are beautiful. I am beautiful. Though I have recognized it in other women for as long as I can remember, I have only begun to see it in myself. Yes, I believe I am beautiful. Some days. Well, some moments. God help us all to believe it more deeply and more often. Because in the places where we don't believe it, we continue to shame ourselves. And shame will never be an agent of change.

trying to fit in

I became a Christian when I was a senior in college and had hit rock bottom. I was a disaster, powerless to change and hopeless that I ever could. I hated myself, hated the choices I had made, the things I had done, and the person I had become. It was misogyny aimed by myself straight at myself—cheered on by the Evil One. In the depths of my brokenness, Jesus whispered longing for himself into my heart.

I really love my testimony. I love the miracle of it and the role my husband played in it. I was home from college one weekend, and John came over for a visit and told me of his coming to faith in Christ. Now this was huge news. I knew that John had been seeking spiritually for years, but he seemed to be seeking only in the most, shall we say, unconventional ways. His faith in Jesus was the biggest turnaround I had ever seen. Spiritually hungry myself, I loved hearing John talk about God and the Bible. My spirit quickened, and over a period of months I gave my heart and my life to Jesus as well.

But back at college John remained the only Christian I knew, and he lived two and a half hours away.

I knew I needed people of faith in my life, and I knew of only one place to find them. In the quad area of the university I attended, clubs set up tables advertising their events and recruiting members. I had seen a large table many times with a sign on it that irked my militant feminist heart. "Fishers of Men," it read. Campus Crusade for Christ had a table inviting people to sign up for Bible studies. I really hated that sign. What about *women*?

But I was desperate. I stealthily approached the table, moving from post to post, gaining the courage to sign up to be in a Bible study. The woman behind the table was very kind, very warm. She was also wearing polyester plaid pants and a polyester knit top. Honestly, to me she looked like she had just stepped out of *Leave It to Beaver*, and I looked like the hippy I was: gauze skirt, Birkenstocks, unshaven legs, and Indian top. (What happened to that top? It was awesome.)

The point of this story is what I believed about myself while meeting this woman for the first time. I saw her and thought, *I'm going to have to dress like that now*. I believed that in becoming a Christian I needed to lay down who I was. More than simply laying down what I did, I thought I had to turn my back on what I liked, my tastes, my desires, my heart. After all, weren't they all sinful?

I was serious about my Jesus. He had grabbed hold of my heart and I had grabbed hold of his, and like a drowning woman clinging to a life preserver, I was not going to let go. If that meant I changed how I dressed completely, then so be it. If that meant I killed or ignored everything about me, then fine.

Now, part of our sanctification does mean we change. We let go of aspects of ourselves, even the ways we dress that don't make God happy or reflect who we really are as his beloved. We don't dress immodestly, because we are precious and holy and deeply loved. We don't cheat on our taxes or steal from the grocery store or spend our Friday nights drinking until we pass out. But we do grow increasingly into who we uniquely are in Christ.

However, I abandoned something else, something essential to me. By so readily abandoning my likes and dislikes, I came to not trust my intuition.

I buried what I was drawn to and instead took all my cues from others. How I dressed. What to give as a birthday present. Which pillow to buy for the chair. What color to paint the room. Putting on spiritual and emotional Spanx, I tried to squeeze myself into what I believed was a more acceptable form.

I didn't just lose myself in Christ. I rejected myself.

And that's the opposite of what Jesus does.

embracing

People are weird. Well, I'm not—but everyone else is. The definition of normal for most of us is "me." It is actually helpful to acknowledge the truth that we are just as quirky as everyone else and that God loves quirky! He loves you! He has a fabulous sense of humor, and he adores yours. (He always gets your jokes even if no one else does!)

He made you *you*—on purpose. You are the only you—ever. Becoming ourselves means we are actively cooperating with God's intention for our lives, not fighting him or ourselves. God accepts us right at this moment, and he wants us to accept ourselves as well. He looks at us with pleasure and with mercy, and he wants us to look at ourselves with pleasure and mercy too! Accepting who we are includes accepting and being thankful for our imperfect bodies, but it isn't limited to that. We can accept other truths about ourselves. Our personality is our own. Our story is our own. Our taste is our own. The way we have chosen to self-protect is ours. We have a style of relating, a kind of sin we easily fall prey to, and a favorite way to spend a free afternoon. We already are ourselves. Unique. (Cookie cutters only work well for cookies.)

God not only accepts us, he embraces us. Embracing ourselves is a stretch for most of us, but consider: Jesus commands us to love our neighbor as we love ourselves. How can we love our neighbor as ourselves if we do not love ourselves? How can we become joyful women if we are unable to see the humor in our own folly? We do become even more ourselves as we repent of areas in our lives that have nothing to do with faith or love, but God does not live in a perpetual state of disappointment over who we are. Berating ourselves for our flaws and our weakness only serves to undermine our strength to become.

Repenting from our sin is essential.

Beating ourselves up for sinning is no longer an option.

Embracing ourselves has nothing to do with arrogance or settling for a lower version of who we are. Embracing ourselves has everything to do with embracing the goodness of God's creative work in us. It means trusting God, believing that all he has made is glorious and good. And that includes us. You are the only one who can be you. The world, the kingdom of God, and all those around you need you to embrace who you are created to be as you become more fully your *true* self.

So who are you? Well, a great way to discover the answer to that is simply to ask, what do you like? What would you do with your life if you were free to do anything at all?

dreaming with God

When I was a little girl, I dreamed of riding the range with the sheriff, bringing justice to the West and rounding up the bad guys. I can still see what I imagined I would be wearing: a white leather skirt and a white vest edged with fringe. I also had on matching white cowboy boots and a white hat. Yee haw!

And since I am being honest, I might as well confess that I am one of those people who used to practice her Academy Award acceptance speech in front of the mirror. Standing at the bathroom sink, thirteen years old, I practiced looking both humble and startled. "I just want to thank all the little people who brought me here."

I've let those desires go. They have grown and shifted but remain expressions of the same core desire. I no longer dream of being a movie star or riding the range, but I do long to make an impact. I do long for Justice.

About fourteen years ago in a small group, John shared some thoughts about desire, that core place in our hearts where God speaks, and then he invited us to write down what we wanted. To write a long list. Not to edit it. Nothing was too small or large to write down. My list turned out to be two pages long and had things on it as varied as the garden I wanted to nurture, the hope to ride horses with my husband, the healing I longed for a few dear ones to experience, and the wedding of a single friend I wanted to dance at.

I found that list a few years ago, and to my astonishment every single item had come true. It had happened!

I needed to make a new list! I have. Don't you want to be on it?

God dreams big. And he invites us to dream big with him. God has planted dreams and desires in each one of our hearts, and they are unique to us. Opening up our spirits, our minds, our heart, our imaginations to what we would really like—to even the possibility of wanting—allows the Holy Spirit to awaken parts of ourselves that are in such a deep sleep no dreams are happening.

God is a Dreamer. He has dreams of you and for you.

When we dream with God, we don't want to run to thinking, *How can I make this happen?* Dreaming with God isn't about *how*. It's about what. If anything could happen, then what would I love to see happen in my life? What would I love to see happen in the lives of those I love? It's really much easier to dream for other people, to have desires for our children and our friends. We can fairly easily name what we want their lives to look like, the healing and the freedom we'd love for them to come to know. It's a wee bit more difficult to dream for our own lives.

But this book is about *your* heart. This moment is about your dreams and your desires that contribute to the unique, marvelous woman you are. The point is not so much being able to name the desire as it is to allow God to access the places in our hearts where dreams and desires are planted. God speaks to us there. About himself. About ourselves.

It's okay to want, and it's okay to want *more*. Wanting more has nothing to do with being unsatisfied or lacking in your present reality. It's being open to the more that God wants to bring to you in your own life. The possibilities for you are limitless! They are. Yes, they are. Maybe not for tomorrow but for your *life*.

What is pushing it with God? What can't he do? What is too hard for him to accomplish in your relationships, your achievements, your creativity, in the fullness of the expression of who you are? We want to be women who are continuing to grow all our lives. We never want to stop. Yes, we rest. But a heart alive is a heart that is awake and curious and pressing in to more.

what do you *want*?

People who regularly write down their dreams and desires earn nine times as much over their lifetimes as people who don't. Most Americans (80 percent) say they don't have any dreams, and we can imagine why. Life can suck the dreaming right out of you. The living God wants to pour those dreams back in. Sixteen percent of Americans say they do have dreams, but they don't write them down. Four percent have dreams and desires, and write them down, but less than 1 percent review and update them on a regular basis.[1]

It is the people who allow themselves to dream, who own their dreams, who write them down and look at them periodically, whose life dreams are coming true.

It's good to dream. We can't out-give God. We can't out-love him, and we can't out-dream him. Give yourself permission to dream big! Dream deep. Dream wide.

Because the thing about dreams is, *dreams come true.*

I have dreams today that are large and varied. On my list are things like: I want to grow tomatoes in a pot and make an amazing *tres leches* cake. I want to be able to get on a horse without using a block. I want to write a book for women, and I want it to be really helpful to many. There are people I want to see come to Christ, countries I want to travel to and minister in, and a size I want to wear.

I have longings and dreams for my husband and for my sons and for our relationships. I want to learn to take really good pictures and capture the beauty that captures my eye. I want to be strong. I want to know the heart of God intimately. I want his life to fill me and flow through me powerfully and joyfully. I want to find out how deeply I can dive into the vastness of his love—how much of his heart can I know?

There are some dreams that come true here, on this side of heaven. As in, I'm pretty sure that one day I am going to be able to grow tomatoes. And there are some that will simply continue to unfold, like really knowing the heart of God.

I encourage you to risk dreaming and writing your dreams down. Once you get started, you'll find there are things you want. And if you can't get started, another approach is simply to begin listing the things you like. What do you *like*? From coffee to the fragrance of lilacs to a comforter before a fire to karaoke, it's a nourishing discipline simply to become aware of what you enjoy and to write it down.

It's good to sit with God in the quiet and ask him to reveal to you: what do I want? And ask him, what do *you* want for me? I do know that one of the things he wants is your heart to become more alive, more awake, and more aware of your own inner workings and his pleasure over who you are. Today. Right in this moment. *Who you are* fleshes out in *what you want*.

Awakening and owning the dreams that God has placed in our hearts isn't about getting stuff or attaining something. It's about embracing who we are and who he has created us to be. In him. He is our dream come true, and the one true love of our life. But we can't love him with our whole hearts when our hearts are asleep. To love Jesus means to risk coming awake, to risk wanting and desiring.

Writing down your dreams and desires is good and is just between you and God. You can share your dreams with someone in your life who you know will handle your heart well, but you don't have to. Let your want-o-meter go off the charts. It is not even remotely connected to your dissatisfied-o-meter.

There is a reason you have the desires you do. Some desires you share with many others. Many people want the same core, good things: a community, a relationship, a deeper walk with God. But many of your dreams and desires are yours alone. They have been given to you by God for you to awaken to, embrace, nurture, pursue, and then offer. Let God use your dreams to guide you into the fuller expression of your unfolding glorious self!

We need to increasingly live from the fullness of our whole hearts in order to become who we are meant to be and play the significant role that is ours to play. We want to be awake and alert. We want to be women who *live their lives on purpose.*

God gives us our dreams, and we give them back to him. By dreaming and writing them down, we aren't demanding they come true. We are just owning the reality that they are a part of us. And since they are a part of us, we embrace them.

> *Jesus, come. Guide me. Holy Spirit, fill me. Dream with me*
> *and in me. Help me to unlock the desires you have planted*
> *in my heart and to write them down. Help me to dream big.*

Ask yourself:

What would I love to do? What would I love to experience or create or offer?

What do I want to be really good at?

What do I want with God? What does God want with me?

What do I want to be known for?

Nothing is impossible with God. Nothing is too good to be true. And besides, if you don't have a dream, how can you have a dream come true?

my pants

A few years ago I came home from a hair appointment, and honestly my hair looked fantastic. I don't know what my hairdresser does, but the day she does my hair, it's amazing. I can never replicate it. On this particular day I looked in the mirror and saw fabulous hair, and I felt pretty. I *felt* pretty. We all know that can be a rare occurrence!

I had a meeting to go to in a couple of hours, so I changed into more work-appropriate attire: a pair of nicer jeans. I love these jeans. I don't know what it is about them, but they work. I put on a red top and big turquoise earrings. Not my usual go-to outfit, but I loved it.

As soon as I was dressed, a friend dropped by unexpectedly, and when she saw me she stopped dead in her tracks and exclaimed, "You are inhabiting your beauty!"

I was inhabiting my beauty. I had worn the jeans before, the top before, and probably the earrings with them, but something in my spirit had relaxed and I was embracing being myself, a woman who believed God when he said, "You are lovely."

My friend left and John came home, and he had the same reaction to me that my friend did, and let's just say that the outfit came off and had to come back on again before the meeting. (It's okay. We're *married*! It's a good thing!)

I wasn't squeezing into the pants by the use of an elastic torture device, nor was I squeezing my soul into any other prescribed form. Rather, I was inhabiting my beauty, just being me and embracing who that is. It might have been for the first time, but please Jesus, not for the last. Some reading this may say, "Those jeans must be amazing and looked really great on you, but I don't look good in any pair of jeans."

Can I just tell you that those jeans are a size 24? Those fabulous, awesome, man-I-love-these-pants are a size 24. I can be fully dressed these days and pull them on over my clothes, and they drop to the ground. I am no longer a size 24, but I pray to inhabit my beauty as well as I did on that monumental day. On every level.

I was recently at a church luncheon for the women's ministry, and one table was filled with older women. Two were ninety, and one was celebrating her ninety-third birthday that very day. Their hair was coiffed, and they were dressed so nicely, makeup applied, and having so much fun I just wanted to be at their table. To say that our beauty as women peaks somewhere in our twenties is laughably absurd. Yes, there is a vibrant beauty to youth, but *these* women—these much older women—were stunning.

They had wrinkles and gray hair. No Botox or lip filler or liposuction could erase their years. But they had something else much more beautiful than youth. They had hearts that had been cultivated by faith over decades. They had a light shining from their eyes that all the sorrow and pain and loss they had undoubtedly endured could not extinguish. They loved God and their hearts were alive and there is nothing more gorgeous than that.

God says our latter glory will exceed our former. To our great loss, in our society we no longer value the wisdom and expertise that comes through living well through many years. Silver hair and wrinkles are earned.

I have learned that being beautiful, feeling lovely, and enjoying who we uniquely are have absolutely nothing to do with our weight, our age, or the shape of our bodies. Take that in a moment and try it on for size. Let the possibility of that being true settle into your spirit for a moment before you quickly dismiss the idea. Beauty is not about the hair, the clothes, the marital status, the bank account, or the number on the scale. Being beautiful is a quality of spirit recognized primarily in a woman whose soul is at rest because she believes her God when he calls her lovely. She is no longer striving to reach the world's unattainable standards of beauty and acceptance but instead is receiving the inheritance that is hers as an image bearer of the living God. She is embracing who God has made her to be.

You are a stunner. And the more you grow in knowing God, the more you will love him, and the more his life and his beauty will inhabit you and flow out from your unique, fabulous, embraceable self.

Go ahead and take a good long look in the mirror. Tell yourself you are a knockout. God says you are, and well, he ought to know.

7

from fear to desire

We have to be braver than we think we can be, because
God is constantly calling us to be more than we are.
—Madeleine L'Engle

Fear not!
—Jesus

One night when I was in college I came home alone to my dark apartment, unlocked the door, walked in, and slammed it shut behind me. After I took several steps I began to feel that something was off. I looked back, and there in the shadows behind the door, shrouded by the night, was a man. I didn't scream. I didn't run. I didn't even move. My legs simply turned into Jell-O, and I collapsed onto the floor. Great to know what I do in a life-threatening situation. I've always been a little disappointed by my petrified reaction. Still, fear will do that to a person. (The man turned out to be my roommate's boyfriend playing a joke on me. And yes, he felt terrible for it.)

In that moment when fear gripped me, I was utterly powerless. Have you ever had those awful dreams where you need to cry out to save someone or to save yourself—and for the life of you, you can't utter a sound? Or you need to get away, but your legs feel frozen and you cannot move, cannot run? We've all had those dreams. They are horrible.

Fear paralyzes. Fear in its mildest, tamest form is a party pooper. It is a wet blanket that smothers the fiery passion God deposited in your heart when he formed you. Fear freezes us into inaction. Frozen ideas, frozen souls, frozen bodies can't move, can't dream, can't risk, can't love, and can't live. Fear chains us.

beauty vs. fear

You probably know the famous passage directed toward women by the old apostle Peter. It is a passage normally used to discuss true inner beauty:

> Your beauty should not come from outward adornment, such as elaborate hairstyles and the wearing of gold jewelry or fine clothes. Rather, it should be that of your inner self, the unfading beauty of a gentle and quiet spirit, which is of great worth in God's sight. For this is the way the holy women of the past who put their hope in God used to adorn themselves. They submitted themselves to their own husbands, like Sarah, who obeyed Abraham and called him her lord. You are her daughters if you do what is right and do not give way to fear. (1 Pet. 3:3–6 NIV 2011)

Notice that the core of the passage is not beauty per se, but how to get to true beauty, which is this: do not give way to fear. Women are particularly vulnerable to fears of all kinds because we care, because we love, because in God's gracious design we are vulnerable and gloriously so. Our vulnerability is part of what makes us women; it enables us to love as we do, to protect relationship as we do, to comfort and offer mercy, to bring a creative eye to the world. And yes, it also makes us vulnerable to fear.

Fear is defined as *a vital response to physical and emotional danger*. If we were unable to feel it, we wouldn't protect ourselves from legitimate threats. So fear can have its place. God invites us to live in reality. God doesn't want us living a fantasy life or a life of denying reality, like Cleopatra, the queen of Denial. God wants us to live a life where we continually grow in wisdom: "The fear of the LORD is the beginning of wisdom" (Prov. 9:10). There is a good fear, a holy fear, a fear that makes you want to honor and do homage to the one who deserves it. The fear that gets us into the most trouble is not fearing God, but fearing people.

"The fear of man lays a snare" (Prov. 29:25 ESV). That is the fear that keeps us silent when we would be better off speaking. It's the fear of women's committees or going against the grain, and it's the fear that keeps us from saying what the Holy Spirit prompts us to say because we are afraid of what could happen if we do. The fear of man is the fear we are all well acquainted with. The fear of looking or sounding stupid and then being dismissed, expelled, shunned. That's the fear known to every elementary, middle school, and high school student alive. It keeps young men belting their pants below their knees and propels young girls to make choices they later regret. The fear of man is behind the yes being said to every life-stealing, peer-pressuring, large and small personal death.

fear is an enemy

Fear in its most wicked, powerful form cripples our souls and warps the very fabric of our true hearts. It reshapes our inner reality until we bear no resemblance to the dream that is us, to who we *really* are. And our lives bear no resemblance to the lives we are meant to be living. Fear robs us of our very selves.

Ultimately, fear is the domain of Satan and his minions, and it is *massively marketable*. Horror movies have gone from the semi-innocent days of the first *Frankenstein* to the cult genre of absolute terror—bloody, gory, and playing on fear. And people love them. They love the rush of feelings they evoke.

> The horror DVD is the top choice for many people when it comes to selecting a film.... Perhaps the most obvious reason why horror films are so popular is because people like to watch them at Halloween. At a time when everyone is talking about ghosts, witches and unexplained occurrences, people like to put on a horror DVD and get in the spirit.[1]

Yes, you can get into the spirit of Halloween by watching a horror movie, but sometimes that spirit gets into you—literally. The Enemy loves to use fear, and you do not want to be opening your life to spirits of fear, for heaven's sake. Haven't we enough to deal with? Feeling fear is not a good thing. Yet all of us still have places where fear has a hold on us.

Fear is also defined as "a distressing emotion aroused by impending danger, evil, or pain; whether the threat is real or imagined; the feeling or condition of being afraid."[2]

Others define it this way:

> F.E.A.R.: Faith Exits and Runs
> F.E.A.R.: Forget Everything and React

Or the ever popular:

> F.E.A.R.: False Evidence Appearing Real

Yet often the evidence that appears real *is* real. There may be a man standing behind the door. There are car accidents. Horrible, tragic things do happen. And you may never see them coming until they are upon you. You know this personally. And you can quickly put two and two together—if such tragedy could befall that family, who knows what could happen to ours? If *this* bad thing can happen, then *that* even worse thing could happen too.

We women are fleet of foot when it comes to running down trails of fear and speculation. Really now—you have a recurring headache. How quickly do you jump to, *Maybe it's a brain tumor; maybe I'm dying*? Your best friend doesn't call; several days go by without a call. Do you jump to, *She's mad at me; I offended her; she's probably talking with someone else now; I've been replaced*. Most of my friends confess to this. I confess to it!

How in heaven's name do we keep fear from dominating our lives?

let's be honest

I am well aware of who I'm speaking to. I know a good many of the stories of the women who will be reading these pages, and I take my shoes off. You who have suffered so much are living proof of the amazing, unsurpassable beauty and goodness, grace and strength, of our God. I don't mean to be brazen here. I want to be tender with your heart, tender with the story of your life. I just want to be firm, *very firm*, with fear.

In order to overcome fear, we first have to be honest about life on this planet.

We fear that our marriage will not last. It may not. We fear that we may lose something or someone precious to us, and we may. We fear being embarrassed if we speak up or fall down or come out of the bathroom trailing toilet paper. (A gal I worked with a number of years ago came out of the bathroom with her skirt tucked into her panty hose. She walked by her male boss and several male coworkers before making the discovery. Oh dear. It was so much worse than trailing toilet paper.) Things happen. Little things. Huge things. The truth is, on any given day, we do not know what is coming our way.

Honestly, we live in a world that seems to only be getting worse. We watch the news or walk outside, and it looks as if the world is going to hell on a greased pole. It is sometimes a dangerous, dark place. We are living in a fallen world, and we are women who love. So we are vulnerable. When you love, you are vulnerable to loss, exposure, abandonment, and your worst fears coming true. When you love someone, you risk losing them. You risk enduring every painful thing we'd much rather avoid.

Abandonment

Betrayal

Illness

Death

Sorrow

Grief

Depression

Division

Rejection

And that's just the short list. We fear failure in life, failure *at* life. Failure in relationship. Like many women, my deepest fear is that something terrible will happen to my husband or my sons. What is yours?

The hard, true thing about our deepest fears is that what happens is completely out of our control. Life is primarily out of our control. People are out of our control, and certainly their choices are out of our control. There is only one person we can ultimately choose life over fear for. Ourselves.

fear is not our friend

I know fear can be a motivator, like the fear of having no friends who stick around because you realize you can be completely self-centered. That may compel you to learn how to not talk all the time. To ask questions of others. To actually wait and listen to their answers. That's a good thing. Or you fear you are stuck personally, so you see a counselor, or stuck professionally, so you take a class or seek a mentor. Fear can motivate in good ways like an adrenaline rush causing you to run for safety.

But fear is never a lasting agent of change any more than shame is. It won't see us through to life on the other side. If unaddressed it will simply attempt to make peace with us. "It's *normal* to be afraid of this or that. It's *fine*." Or it will morph, but usually it will spread. Once it has a hold on a certain area of your life, fear will do its best to increase its hold to more places.

You know what we do as women when we feel afraid: we reach for control.

We do it in relationship when we self-protect. But when we choose to protect ourselves in fear and withdraw, we have already lost everything. We are already alone. Self-protecting is not our ally. As Beth Moore said at a conference I attended in 2008, "We can self-protect ourselves right out of our calling." We can self-protect ourselves right out of our becoming, right out of the will of God. God is a God of love, and we are commanded to love as well. Do not fear! Love!

I'm a mother. My life and my heart are out running around hither and yon completely out of my control. I have risk-taking, adventure-loving, passionate sons who prefer cliff jumping to stamp collecting, motorcycles to minivans, and rock climbing to studying coins. I am pretty aware of the world we live in, both the physical and spiritual realities. I am acquainted with fear. Too many times I have tried to ease my fears by reaching for control over my husband, my sons, and my world. It almost always made things worse.

I got a call from a friend asking me for some advice or at least for my eyes on her relationship with her teenage son. He had recently said to her, "You need to back off." Her husband later told her, "You basically have your foot on his throat." She was controlling him. Pushing him to talk. Bringing up the subjects of drugs and alcohol and safety and godliness again and again and again. She wasn't inviting him to conversation but demanding that he listen. Out of—you guessed it—fear. She wanted to keep him close and safe. It was having the opposite effect. She learned that through her fear-based actions she was pushing him away.

Parameters are good. Conversations are good. Instruction is good. We are right to control our children and teach them about safety and choices and the world in which they live and, as they mature, to give them increasing amounts of freedom. We lengthen the leash that's attached to our hip and then let it go. And when we can't do that, the issue is fear. But the deeper issue is *trust*.

Can we trust our lives, our futures, and the lives of those we love to God? Can we trust a God we can't control? Can we trust this God whose take on life and death and suffering and joy is so very different from our own?

Yes. Yes, we can.

Because we know him. And we know he is good.

only love

We have fears below the surface that we don't consciously know we have. God wants us to be free *of* them. How can we be? Well, he has made a way for us. It is the way of his love. His perfect love for us casts out all fear.

> And so we know and rely on the love God has for us.
> God is love. Whoever lives in love lives in God, and
> God in them…. There is no fear in love. But perfect love

drives out fear.... The one who fears is not made perfect
in love. (1 John 4:16, 18 NIV 2011)

We have to choose life. Choose risk. Choose love. The only safe
place for our hearts is to dive deeply into the magnificent, eternal,
ridiculous, overwhelming love that God has for us. His love is the only
safety net that will hold. Really, do you have an option? How is that life
of fearful control working for you? Better to ask, how is it working for
those who have to live with your fearful control? Come and be free in
the love of God.

I'm not making idle religious promises here. We do have a couple of
guarantees in this life as Christians, but maybe not as many as we would
like. Becoming a Christian does not guarantee a painless life. It doesn't
mean that we will be safe from tragedy, loss, or sorrow. But it does mean
that in it and through it, *we will be all right*. Actually we will be much better
than all right. Though we don't have all the control and assurance we may
want, we as God's beloved can be certain of many things.

We can be pretty sure we are going to die. (You may be holding out
that Jesus is going to come back before you die, but one way or the other,
we are all leaving this place.) The average life span for women in the United
States is seventy-eight years. It's a little less for men. All of us at one time or
another are going to leave this world as we know it. We can be sure of that.
But we don't need to fear it because we can be certain of what is coming
next. Eternal life is real. Heaven is real. Some of those we love so deeply
have already gone on before us, and the pain of losing them is comforted
by the fact that we have not lost them forever. We are parted now for a little
while. A sweet reunion is coming. We are promised that.

We know that we are more than conquerors through him who loves
us. We know that nothing, nothing, *nothing* will be able to separate us
from the love of God that is in Christ Jesus our Lord. And we know that in

all things God works for the good of those who love him, who have been called according to his purpose. All things. Even the other shoe dropping. We are promised that.

We are promised that we will never be alone. Jesus promises that he will never leave us or forsake us or turn his face away no matter what our emotions or circumstances are telling us. And we are promised that we will have everything we need. *Everything*.

Paul says in Philippians 4:19, "And my God will meet all your needs according to his glorious riches in Christ Jesus." Our needs won't be met according to the destitution of the world or to the poverty of our own faith in the moment but according to the riches in Jesus. There's no one richer than him!

Now, I admit that what I sincerely believe I need doesn't always line up with what God believes I need. But all of us have stories of God coming through when we needed him most. From groceries left on my doorstep, to an anonymous gift of twenty dollars that allowed me to put gas in my car, to the tuition for college supplied on the date it was due, I have amazing stories.

Our God is the God of last-minute deliverances. But his view is different from ours. Jeremiah was set apart in his mother's womb to be a prophet and told by God not to fear: "'They will fight against you but will not overcome you, for I am with you and will rescue you,' declares the LORD" (Jer. 1:19).

That promise was fulfilled many times in the biblical narrative. But Jeremiah was attacked by his own brothers, beaten and put into the stocks by a priest and false prophet, imprisoned by the king, threatened with death, thrown into a cistern by Judah's officials, and opposed by a false prophet.

Ummmm. When did God rescue him exactly? After he was beaten. After he was imprisoned. After he was threatened, opposed, and thrown into a cistern. Yes, God's view is dramatically different from ours. Jeremiah went through much travail. So has every saint before him and after him, though not all to that extreme. And regardless of what comes our way, God tells all of us, "Don't be afraid." He says, "My grace is sufficient for you."

A friend recently shared this wisdom: "Love displaces fear, so in order to truly become so fearless that you can live out the way of life God has for you, you will have to become so immersed in the presence of love that there is no room for fear. Courage comes from love, never from fear."

We want to be women who advance. The kingdom of God is advancing, and the gates of hell will not prevail against it. Don't you want to advance along with it? Don't you want to help it to advance? And don't you want to advance into the deeper realms of the heart of God? Advance into more healing, more deliverance, more intimacy, more life? Fear makes us retreat. Love causes us to advance.

don't be afraid

I love the story of Jairus and Jesus found in Mark 5. Jesus had just crossed over the lake, and Jairus—a leader in the synagogue—had gone down to meet him. Actually, he didn't just go down to meet him; he went down to fall at his feet. He asked Jesus—no, he pleaded with him, "My little daughter is dying. Please come and put your hands on her so that she will be healed and live" (v. 23). And Jesus, being fully himself, said sure. You remember the story.

Jesus was walking to Jairus's house, but he didn't go alone. A crowd went with him. He was being jostled, pushed against, pressed into when suddenly he stopped and asked the seemingly ridiculous question, "Who touched me?"

A woman came forward. She too fell at his feet and told him, the Scriptures say, "the whole truth" (v. 33). She had been bleeding for twelve years. She was getting worse. She had seen every doctor, done every treatment, and spent every dime. She knew only that if she could press through the crowds and even just touch Jesus's garment, she would be healed.

It was illegal for this woman to be out with the people. She was bleeding. She was unclean. It was against the law that she, a woman, would touch Jesus, a man. But against all the laws and against all the odds, she reached out to Jesus, she pressed into him with everything she had, and she was healed.

And Jesus thought she was awesome. "Your faith has healed you. Go in peace" (v. 34). He recognized her as one of his own. He called her daughter.

Daughter, Jesus recognizes you as well. His face is turned toward you in kind intent. You can come to him with your whole story. Everything you are as a woman and everything you are not. You can bring him your victories and your failures and your fears. He will withhold no good thing from you. He will not turn his face away.

After the woman was healed and went on her joyous way, a servant came to meet Jairus and told him that his daughter had died. "Why bother the teacher anymore?" Jesus turned to Jairus and spoke the very same words he is speaking to us today: "Don't be afraid; just believe" (v. 36).

In the face of the impossible, Jesus told Jairus (and tells us) to hope. With the words spoken that Jairus's worst fear had come true, Jesus said, "Don't give in to fear. You may not see the way, but with me nothing is impossible. I am good. You can trust me."

Jairus did not leave Jesus then. Jairus continued to press on with him to his home and invited Jesus to his dead daughter's bedside. Somewhere deep inside Jairus, a spark of hope had flared that even his deepest fear coming true could not quench.

And you know what happened next. Jesus said to the little girl, "Get up." So she did. Who could possibly resist the call of Jesus?

desire awakens

A couple of years ago on my morning walk and time with God, and after many years of praying for this, I felt the cement blocks of fear I have carried in my heart around the lives of my sons fall off. Just fall *off*. It was one of those instances when the veil between heaven and earth is so very thin. In those moments, I know the goodness of God, the surety of heaven, the power and authority of being Jesus's, and in that particular moment, the truth that I had absolutely nothing to fear on behalf of my boys or my husband. Or me. Nothing.

It was such a great feeling.

As soon as the weight came off, where my thoughts went next really surprised me. I felt a freedom to *want*. The desire to skydive reemerged. That would be awesome. (Where had that gone?) The desire surfaced to ride bikes and climb mountains and have dinner parties and know Jesus like crazy and teach women and speak at arenas and *live my life*. Fully. With abandon.

I am letting you in on a wonderful secret.

What happens when God comes and releases us from long-held fears or fears that have long held us? What happens when we surrender fear to God and invite his love to overwhelm it? What is on the other side of fear? Is it faith? Yes, but the form it takes is desire. What comes is a surfacing of *desire*. Or perhaps a resurfacing of desire.

Desires surface that you didn't even know you had. Freedom rises to embrace your life and live it. I mean really live it. To live unabashedly. Desires rise in your heart for yourself and for others. Desires awaken regarding what you want to offer, do, experience, *become*. No longer bound by fear, how high can we soar? How deep can we dive? How much delight can we experience? Yes, there will be sorrow too—it's a part of the deal—but life gets the final word. *Life*. Life always gets the final word. Every single time. Forever.

Praise the LORD, O my soul;

all my inmost being, praise his holy name.

Praise the LORD, O my soul,

and forget not all his benefits—

who forgives all your sins

and heals all your diseases,

who redeems your life from the pit

and crowns you with love and compassion,

who satisfies your desires with good things

so that your youth is renewed like the eagle's.

(Ps. 103:1–5)

give your fears to Jesus

Fear is not our ally. It is not our destiny. As Franklin Roosevelt said, "The only thing we have to fear is fear itself." The things we fear are in the way of our coming closer to Jesus, receiving his love, and being perfected by his love. We want to allow God to reveal what fears we have that we may not even know we have, and then we want to respond by raising the white flag of surrender. Surrender. Not to the fear. But to God. To his love. To allow his perfect love to cast out fear and then to receive what he desires for us instead.

You probably know what you have been afraid to entrust to God. When we surrender our fear, we are offering it to Jesus. We are saying, "This fear is too much fear for me to bear. I give it to you because I believe you are good and worthy of my trust." When we actively, by faith, lay down our fears at the feet of Jesus, we pick up his love in return. It is an uneven trade, a heavenly exchange.

This past year was a very difficult one for John and me. We faced a great deal of spiritual attack, and at one point it was so severe I thought

John might lose his life. I was *afraid*. One night John came into the living room and said, "We have got to take this weapon out of the Enemy's hand. He is using fear against us. Fear about me." We talked about the passage in Revelation 12 that says the saints overcome the Evil One "by the blood of the Lamb and by the word of their testimony; they did not love their lives so much as to shrink from death" (v. 11). No fear—especially about death.

John and I knelt down. We confessed our fears to Jesus. We gave him total control over our lives, including the timing of our deaths. We renounced fear, and we made peace with the fact that our lives are in God's hands. It was a turning point for us; the fear really lost its brutal grip.

Laying down what we want to protect or are afraid of losing or are terrified we will never have is not the same thing as losing those things. It is *surrendering* them. It is opening up our clenched hand around them and allowing God access to them and to us. It is actually saying yes to God for them. Yes to his plan. Yes to his way. It is believing that just as his ways are higher than the heavens are above the earth, so his way for the things we fear is higher. This God of ours is a God of life, of goodness. He is the God of the Resurrection. We lay down our fear. We pick up Jesus. He is the only way we can live beyond fear. He is the Way.

Take a moment and in the quiet, think of what it is you fear. Ask God to reveal it to you.

> *Jesus, would you please reveal to me what I am so afraid of?*
> *What or who am I not trusting you with? Just help me picture*
> *it, imagine it, see their faces. Lord, I want to trust you. Would*
> *you please help me give you my lingering fear? Come for me*
> *here, Jesus. Please help me. I need you. In your Name. Amen.*

There is no shame here. The places where we still fear are simply the places we have yet to fully receive God's love. Only by his grace and in his love can we let our fear go. Let go and *receive*. Receive his dreams. Receive his love. It is an exchange of fear for desire. It is an exchange of death for life.

There is no fear in love. And I can tell you this with certainty: God does not want you to live in fear. And he does want you to live.

Don't be afraid. Just believe.

8

the company of women

The next best thing to being wise oneself is to live in a circle of those who are.
—C. S. Lewis, *Selected Literary Essays*

I was taking a walk beneath the wide-open Colorado sky. At the height of summer, the warmth embraced me like an old friend. The sky was cloudless, the blue opaque. Above me two hawks were catching the upward drafts and calling to one another with joy. I stopped to watch them, longing to be able to fly myself. *Someday*, I thought. The red-tailed hawks had their world to themselves: an open sky, no other birds of prey, no eagles or crows to trouble them, just endless space beckoning them to do what they do best.

And then they flew right into each other. *Smack!* What? They both must have been startled. The hawks tumbled many feet in the air before recovering. Then they resumed their play. Or maybe it was their practice.

I thought, *Well, it happens.* If you are soaring or practicing or tumbling in the proximity of others, every now and again you will smack into them.

Then a choice must be made. Either resume flying, perhaps a little wiser for the sting, or take your wings and go home. Retreat to the nearest safe perch.

As followers of Christ, we are not called by God to live a life where safety is the highest goal. Nor is comfort. You knew this already. But dang. I still struggle with accepting it.

The highest goal is love. Always. Well then. In order to be loved and to love, we cannot sit this life out. We have to engage with those folks God has brought us. No woman is meant to live her life as a solo act. We need women to help us on our way. Supporting us. Encouraging us. Challenging us. Calling us back onto the dance floor or into the sky to do what we are meant to do and become who we are meant to become.

Men do that for women, and women do that for men. But we women need other women in our lives. We receive things from women that we do not receive from men. And no one knows what it's like to be a woman better than another woman.

friendship is messy

I must admit right off the bat that although I deeply believe we need women in our lives, those relationships can often sting. Like every other relationship, our friendships with women can be hard. I know we need women in our lives, but sometimes, like you, I can be intimidated by their strength, their beauty, their *way*. Sometimes I retreat from them; from their overwhelming presence or their overwhelming need. Sometimes I am overwhelming myself. I am a woman, after all. And a woman is a wondrous creature with a capacity to affect her world beyond measure.

A woman can be strong yet tender. Powerful yet soft. Fierce with the potential to be kind. Wise but sometimes foolish. Romantic. Cynical. Merciful. Wounded. Beautiful. Silly. Nurturing. Mysterious even to herself. Courageous. Odd. Vulnerable. Beaten down through the centuries yet continually rising up generation after generation. Feared and fearsome. Get a group of them together, moving toward the same goal, and power is released. Nations are forged. Justice is spread. The kingdom of God *advances*.

Women are awesome. Yet sometimes getting near them is like approaching a cactus, hugging a porcupine, or taming a skunk. We get pricked and sprayed. We prick and we spray a good bit ourselves. But still, we need women in our lives. Though at times it may be tempting to resign ourselves to a circle of polite and superficial female relationships, it is not a wise thing. We need women with whom we can be honest about the realities of our lives, both the internal and the external realities. We need women friends who offer us truth in return. We need relationships with women in all their manifest forms, but mostly we need to have a few women *friends*.

I have a very dear friend who in her fierce loyalty to me signs many of her cards and emails with "Your forever friend." She writes that to me, fully aware that I am no longer certain such a thing exists on this side of eternity. My heart has become wary, and my friend pushes against my wariness in loving and unyielding proclamations of faithful friendship. In the face of her love, my wary heart is softening. In the face of her consistent offer of relationship, my heart is healing. Friends can wound at times, deeply, yes. But friends can bless, too. Profoundly.

A good friend loves you when you are hilarious and when you are hurting. A true friend loves you when you are being kind and when you are PMS-ing all over the place. They may not love what you are doing, or the dragon you are manifesting, but they love *you*. They know who the true you is, and even in the midst of your living as an imposter to your very self, a friend calls you up and out. A friend sees who you are meant to be and beckons you to rise to the higher version of yourself.

Friendship is a high and holy thing, and a two-way street. Friendships with women are also messy. They are not for the faint of heart.

I have learned a few things about friendships with women over the years, and where I have made mistakes, I have made colossal ones. I'd love to spare you that, as much as possible anyway. What I have learned, I offer to you.

hold your friends loosely, but hold them

Friendship is risky, costly. Friendship is meant to provide a refuge from loneliness, and a respite from self-criticism and the critique of a never-satisfied world. Friendship is a relationship of mutual enjoyment. It is a place where our hearts don't have to work quite so hard to be heard and understood and accepted. Friendship is supposed to offer a taste of what is coming when our souls will be fully known and completely at rest.

But just a taste. I have found that the people I love and who love me deeply are not able to satisfy my insatiable soul in a lasting way. But man, have I wanted them to. "Fill me!" I've cried. "Satisfy me!" John has tried to fill me. Friends have tried to fill me. And their offerings have been marvelous. But never enough. I have a leak. Really, it's a break in the pipe, and, aware of my own brokenness, I have tried to hide it and get other people to tend it. It hasn't worked. My demanding has backfired. I have learned the hard way—and just about everything I have learned, I have learned the hard way—the beautiful freeing truth that Jesus is the only One who can satisfy me. He's actually the only one who is meant to!

Coming to know Jesus more truly as my primary forever Friend is freeing my heart to offer and receive the amazing gift of friendship. Friendship, fellowship, is a gift, one that each of us is meant to enjoy and offer. We need each other. But in order to continue to move toward one another and receive freely what others are meant to share with us, we need Jesus.

Who among us has not suffered betrayal at the hands of a trusted friend? Who among us has not shrunk away in response to being hurt? Which one of us has not been responsible for wounding another? We all have.

We *all* have.

We need Jesus. We need mercy. We need healing. We are not meant to live this life alone, and we won't get very far along on our journey if we try. We don't have the luxury of insisting we never be hurt again. We don't get to insist on anything, really. Except maybe we can insist on continuing to press in to Jesus, no matter what.

He's here. He's waiting. He has never betrayed you, and he never will. He is the Source of our true identity. He is the One we must look to first to fill us with truth, acceptance, and love. Then we can bring our hearts, be they bursting with joy or battered by life, to our friends without demanding that they fill us. We can offer ourselves, open to receive good gifts from them but vigilant to stay close to our God and screening every experience, every word, through him. He has promised to never leave you or forsake you. He is the same yesterday, today, and forever. He is perfect love, and he loves you perfectly. And he's not going anywhere.

Friendships do change. People change. You change. You are supposed to. You may still be walking in the same direction in life as a dear friend, but your paths may no longer cross. Churches split. Bible studies end. Children switch schools. Gyms close. People move. Jobs change. The natural and easy ways that we as friends connect shift under our feet, and it takes enormous effort on *both* sides for the friendship to shift and continue as well. Perhaps it is meant to continue. Perhaps it isn't. Some friends we are called to fight for and some we are called to release.

I was at a Graham Cooke conference a number of years ago when he taught about how our friendships change and how *normal* that is. He said most friendships last three to five years. Really? And, he said, they are *meant to* have a duration of three to five years. Not every friend in our lives is meant to walk with us through the remainder of our lives. Oh, we love them still. And though all change feels like loss, it is good to bless people on their way, to hold them loosely, and to let them go.

The ironic thing is, I was at that Graham Cooke conference with a close friend who I deeply loved and who I was not holding with a loose hand but with a clenched fist. We had been friends for many years, and I assumed we would be friends for the rest of our lives. I ignored the telltale signs of change. This friend had been moving away from me for quite a long while, but I absolutely refused to see it. I wanted what *I* wanted. I thought she was fabulous. Surely she must feel the same way about me!

Somewhere along the way, my desire for relationship turned into demand, and demand is one of the death knells of a friendship—of any relationship, really. I needed to unclench my fist and in love let my friend go. I also needed to invite Jesus into the places of my heart that had refused to see that it was time to let her go.

Insisting. Demanding. Refusing. I promise you, those are not verbs that lead to the life Jesus has for us.

Not every woman or man in your life is going to stay in your life for the duration of it. Not every person you long to have a friendship with is meant to be your friend. (Sorry. Now take a big, deep breath.) It can be excruciating to let a friend go, or worse, to be let go of. Many people underestimate the closeness of heart that women friends are capable of reaching. How well I remember sobbing in the arms of a precious friend when my young family was moving across the country. It felt like my heart was being torn out. And we loved each other. How much worse it is when a friendship ends because of offenses, misunderstandings, anger, or betrayal. How searingly painful it is when God calls you to walk away from a cherished friend when love and unity have left the relationship.

We are meant to grow and change and become throughout the duration of our lives, and we need to be surrounded by people who celebrate the person we are *becoming*. Our true friends are people who are our biggest cheerleaders and encourage us on to the next higher version of ourselves whom God is calling us up to. Friends delight in one another's successes and blessings and are vigilant against jealousy and envy.

Jealousy and envy are two additional death knells to a friendship. God does not want us to be jealous of what a friend receives or achieves. We are called to rejoice with them. We want the best for our friends always and only. Walking with a friend through trials requires much tenderness, grace, and wisdom on our part, but it is actually more difficult to walk with a friend through a season of success and blessing. "We didn't get a vacation like that." "I wish I had been given the opportunity to travel." "I love their new sofa. I wish I had a new sofa." Careful.

It's a challenge. Loving people through travail and success requires much from us. God is always at work sifting and shaping, purifying and clarifying, what is in our hearts. To stay in relationship with another person requires first that we stay in relationship with God. He is the only way we can navigate through jealousies that rear their ugly heads or offenses from others that prick our vulnerable hearts.

Truth be told, a good part of our becoming takes place in the sanctifying work of relationships. And not because friendship is always a greenhouse, either. Trees grow strong because of winds; drought forces their roots to go deeper. There isn't anything on earth like relationships to make you holy. When our frail humanity is revealed in some way we and others don't like, we bring it to God. We ask for forgiveness. We ask for his life to fill us and his love to flow through us. Which means "Christ in me, love through me" becomes a regular prayer.

It always comes back to Jesus. Jesus. Jesus. Jesus.

be careful with your expectations

Sometimes I am absolutely amazed at how much Jesus loves people. Some days—okay, most days—people can be pretty odd. We are all living on the island of misfit toys, and most of us are not even aware that one of our wheels is in the shape of a square. We bump into each other. We step on each other's toes, and then what is one to do?

Friendships can be hard. They are opposed by the Enemy. They need to be fought for. Anything worth having and cherishing is.

For many years, I thought that a cherished best, *best* friend would be a woman who understood me at all times and enjoyed *all* the same things I enjoyed. She'd want to go to a movie when I wanted to go to a movie, and she would want to see the same show I wanted to see. She would be passionately in love with Jesus and desire him above all else and always point my heart back to him. I would do the same for her, and she would think I was amazing and wise and justified in my mood swings. She would be available to me whenever I called and only be encouraging and empathetic. She would vote for the same candidates I vote for. She would always get my jokes and want to eat at the same restaurant I wanted to eat at, and she would never be offended by a failure of mine. Oy! And, yeah, I know, embarrassing, right?

But Oprah has Gayle. Rachel has Monica. Wilma has Betty. Aren't they all that for each other? I'm whining now.

Actually, I am being ridiculous. Because I am a woman blessed in friendship. I have more than my share of amazing friends, friends who are the Best. I am a rich woman. And I am learning that each of these variously gifted women offers something of unique value that the others don't. Their very differences from each other and from me enrich my life! No one woman could possibly be everything to me. God is meeting my need for friendship, just not through one person. Some women are blessed with a best friend. But most women aren't. Most of us have a few friends that provide something we need, and we provide something they need. Our hearts are met in many ways, by the beautiful offerings of a few. I don't think a human being is actually able to bear the burden of being someone's one and only. God alone can be our One and Only.

God understands us all the time. He is available every moment. People don't and aren't. They have lives and schedules and a myriad of people pulling on them, and that makes them normal and not at our beck and call. Jesus calls us "friend." Oh, to know him more deeply as that. I want to know him as my King and my God and my Friend who enjoys me fully, accepts me completely, and loves me unconditionally. Because that is who he is.

Friends are sometimes referred to as "Jesus with skin on," people sharing our humanity and reminding us of the higher truths: there is a God, and he loves us. We need to be reminded. Continually. Left to ourselves, we quickly forget everything that is vital to remember. Solitary confinement is a form of punishment, of torture. Loneliness is a sorrow, separation a grief, and distance painful. Companionship and friendship are human needs, as necessary to our becoming ourselves as air to our lungs and food to our bodies.

be careful with the truth

> *It is important to our friends to believe that we are unreservedly*
> *frank with them, and important to friendship that we are not.*
> —Mignon McLaughlin, *The Complete Neurotic's Notebook*

A word about honesty. The Scripture exhorts us to speak the truth in love. Speak the truth *in love*. Which means, don't speak the truth in anger or resentment or with the desire to wound. We need to be careful to check our motives underneath our speaking the truth. We want to be aware of the "why" behind the desire to share something. We want to know that we are speaking the truth with the desire to love, to bless. A dear friend told me that when we don't speak the truth in love, *it is no longer truth.*

And the Scripture does *not* exhort us to speak everything that is true. In our culture of honesty, we may feel compelled to share everything with our husband or with our close friends, even the negative things. We want to be honest, right? We don't want to have secrets from each other, right? Wrong. To share with one you love or are friends with every thought or emotion that goes through your head wreaks havoc on the relationship. No friendship, no marriage, has the capacity to carry the burdens of our every nuance. Only Jesus does. He knows us. We don't shock him. We are not too much for him. Sharing truth with a friend or a husband in the desire to keep nothing between us can overwhelm the person and the relationship. Good heavens. Of course we don't share everything with our friends. We are tactful. We are honest but only to the point of loving.

I have really blown it here. I once told a good friend about negative feelings I had held about her. I had been jealous of this woman and the close relationship she had with someone that I had wanted to have a close relationship with too. I felt edged out. Three's a crowd and all that. When I realized the unreality of those emotions in the face of the truth—that I loved this woman—I confessed them to her. I told her how untrue those feelings were. I was sorry for them.

Okay, that went over well. Yes, confession is good for the soul, but confession to whom? And good for whose soul? Not to the person you had hurtful thoughts about! Please be shaking your head, saying, "I can't believe Stasi was that stupid to do that." I can't believe it either. But I was. I have asked for forgiveness. But you know as well as I do that words once spoken cannot be unspoken. Wounds can be healed. Damage can be addressed. Forgiveness can be bestowed. Words cannot be erased.

Any relationship, a friendship or a marriage, cannot sustain the brunt of total honesty. Relationships are not meant to be the dumping grounds of every negative thought, belief, or emotion. Let me give you a couple more horrid but true examples.

I was going for yet another walk around our block in Southern California, pushing both my sons in a stroller. My baby was only weeks old, and his brother was months shy of turning two. Our walk was our big outing for the day, unless we had the highlight of going to the grocery store. But most days, John had our one car, and our walk was our wonder.

This day, as I was walking, a woman called to me from the other side of the street from the middle school field. Waving to get my attention, she ran across the street with a teenager. She introduced herself and the unhappy teenage boy she had dragged along with her. She told me he had come to apologize for the insults he had hurled at me the day before when I was walking by, pushing my stroller. She turned to the embarrassed youth and told him it was mean of him to call me a fat slob and an awful collection of other names. He mumbled an apology, I accepted, and—satisfied for seizing her moment—the woman went back across the street with her student.

The thing is, I hadn't heard the young man the day before. The noise of the traffic had muffled his voice, and I had been blissfully unaware of his diatribe. Now I wasn't. Now I was filled with shame. I didn't walk that route again. See, *I didn't need to know.*

Okay. One more. A woman had a close friend who was beginning to soar in her calling. The woman cheered her friend on but became increasingly aware of envy gnawing at her inside. *She* wasn't soaring. *Her* calling was not unfolding in a glorious way like her friend's was. To keep "nothing from separating them," this woman shared with her friend her envy— confessed it and released the burden of it onto her friend.

Why did she do that? Who felt better after the exchange? Who felt worse?

Dear one, they don't need to know everything. When we are struggling with negative emotions, we bring them to Jesus and maybe to a counselor, a pastor, our spouse, or a different trustworthy friend. And when we are through with the negative, separating feelings, we don't dredge them back up and pour them out onto the heart of the one we have finally come to terms with. We can do great damage to one another in the name of "honesty."

As women growing into the fullness of who we are created to be, we speak only the truth that God calls us to speak, in love, and only when he calls us to speak it.

forgive offenses

Misunderstanding one another is so easily and frequently done, it's a miracle any relationship survives. The only way is love. Paul says love "keeps no record of wrongs" (1 Cor. 13:5). In loving relationships, we want to throw away the list in our heads of wrongs done to us and ignore them when they raise their indictments yet again. Too often we keep those lists, ruminate on them, and nurse them like a wounded animal. We say we forgive—and we may even believe we have—but when the list presents itself again we entertain it with a sort of sick satisfaction. "See what they did? Remember what she said?" We have taken the bait of offense. We are inside the trap.

The word used in Scripture for *offense* actually means "bait," the bait that is placed inside a trap to lure an animal to its death.

Offenses need to be forgiven quickly, or they will fester and poison the relationship. The poison seeps out and affects our own souls as well. Offenses that are held on to lead to death.

People will hurt us. We will hurt and offend as well. We all will do this with intention and without, with our thoughts bent to wound and with no thought at all. Jesus took all our offenses into his broken body when he died for us, and he took everyone else's as well. All that he suffered—the beating, the scourging, the mocking, and finally the crucifixion—was more than enough to pay for it all. Our offenses and theirs.

Once when I was reeling from being badly hurt by a person, something wicked rose up in me and I had to admit that, ugly as it was, I wanted them to suffer for it as much as I was suffering. A picture immediately came to my mind of Jesus, tortured and bleeding, and the Holy Spirit asked, "Is this suffering enough?" Yes. Yes, it is. Sometimes in our humanity we may feel that in order for justice to be done, a person needs to pay for their offense. Well, Jesus took their bill. It's been paid for.

With the help of God, we must choose to forgive. Let it go. Let them go. Come out of the trap.

> *Dear God, I forgive all those who have hurt me, and I bless them in Jesus's Name. I pray only more of you to them, for them. And God, I forgive myself for having hurt others. Please fill me with your Spirit and live and love through me that I might become a woman after your heart who loves others well. In Jesus's Name. Amen.*

discern and break unholy ties

"Blest Be the Tie that Binds" is an old hymn celebrating the beauty of Christian fellowship and unity.

> *Blest be the tie that binds*
> *Our hearts in Christian love;*
> *The fellowship of kindred minds*
> *Is like to that above.*

Before our Father's throne
We pour our ardent prayers;
Our fears, our hopes, our aims are one
Our comforts and our cares.

We share each other's woes,
Our mutual burdens bear;
And often for each other flows
The sympathizing tear.[1]

Back during the Jesus Movement of the 1960s and '70s we sang an updated version, "We Are One in the Bond of Love." There are holy and beautiful bonds formed in the body of Christ that come through the Spirit of God. They are bonds of love, bonds created by the Holy Spirit. Living with them is one of the joys of being a Christian! "Make every effort to keep the unity of the Spirit through the bond of peace" (Eph. 4:3).

Sadly, there are unholy bonds as well. Scripture warns against those. For example, "Do not be yoked together with unbelievers. For what do righteousness and wickedness have in common? Or what fellowship can light have with darkness?" (2 Cor. 6:14). So a believer and unbeliever should not marry (though Scripture says if you already are, this is *not* reason to divorce).

Another example of an unholy bond would be sexual relations with people we are not married to: "Do you not know that your bodies are members of Christ himself? Shall I then take the members of Christ and unite them with a prostitute? Never! Do you not know that he who unites himself with a prostitute is one with her in body? For it is said, 'The two will become one flesh'" (1 Cor. 6:15–16).

There is some debate and misunderstanding about whether or not Scripture teaches about "soul ties." Let's try and clear that up. However you want to describe it, the Bible clearly teaches that there are holy and unholy bonds between people. Adam and Eve had a holy bond; they became one. (Clearly this goes way beyond "flesh," as any married couple can tell you, especially those married for many years. The bond is at a soul level as well as physical.) Jonathan and David had a very special bond: "After David had finished talking with Saul, Jonathan became one in spirit with David, and he loved him as himself" (1 Sam. 18:1). The King James Version translates it this way: "the soul of Jonathan was knit with the soul of David." So, bonds between people can clearly be formed.

When Paul warns about being "yoked" with unbelievers, he is describing an unholy bond. When he warns believers not to have sexual relations outside of marriage, he warns against uniting with that person—clearly a type of bond, an unholy bond. But unholy bonds take place outside of sexual relations. You've seen relationships where one woman (or man) holds too much sway over another. The friend and her mother I mentioned in chapter 5 are a good example of an unholy bond; her mother has control over her, and my dear friend has felt powerless to break that bond.

When a mother exerts control over her grown children, there is an illegitimate domination. That is an ungodly soul tie. When a friend controls another through moods or threats (unspoken or spoken), there is an ungodly soul tie present. Given our vulnerability as women, given our deep capacity for relationship, we must be aware of the power of unholy ties.

When someone is worrying about you, angry with you, or judging you, when those emotions cause that person to obsess over you, hold conversations with you when you aren't even present, that creates an unholy bond. This is clearly not the bond of love by the Holy Spirit that Paul says is good; this is an unhealthy bond. These forms of unhealthy ties create all sorts of havoc. They form a kind of spiritual walkway over which another person's warfare travels to you. The negative emotions, demonic strongholds, or accusing spirits that have been accosting them come over and accost you. The soul tie is a two-way street, by the way, so what you are struggling with goes over to them as well.

My mom and I had a massive soul tie. It was more than a walkway; we had the Brooklyn Bridge. After speaking on the phone with my mother, I would often feel overwhelmed, diminished, and even angry. Slowly, I realized (or my husband would point out to me) that what I was feeling (and hadn't been feeling prior to the phone call) was exactly what my mother felt. She was often overwhelmed, diminished, and angry … and only too happy that I would share this with her. But these weren't my feelings at all! I needed to break the soul tie with my mom.

Many years ago, John and I were intervening passionately in a friend's life. His world was crashing down. We both spent many hours counseling him and praying for him and his family. After a couple of weeks, what I can only describe as a darkness, a heaviness, and a weight of despair fell on our household. It was new, strong, and awful. That is when we began to learn about soul ties. We had been fighting for our friend, contending in the spiritual realm on his behalf—but in our own strength. We had formed a soul tie, and all the warfare and heaviness that he was struggling under came barreling into our home.

With some people it feels as if they are sucking the life out of you. That is because they *are* sucking the life out of you. There is an ungodly tie there. You need to break it.

Galatians 6:14 declares that through the cross of Christ, "the world has been crucified to me, and I to the world." The cross changes every relationship. Even family ties. "Anyone who loves their father or mother more than me is not worthy of me; anyone who loves their son or daughter more than me is not worthy of me. Whoever does not take up their cross and follow me is not worthy of me" (Matt. 10:37–38 NIV 2011). All ties are subject now to the rule of Christ. And so we can say, in a very godly and healthy way, "I am crucified to the world, and the world is crucified to me. I am crucified to my mom, to my sister, to my friend, and to my enemy, and they are crucified to me."

The only bond we are urged to maintain is the bond of love by the Holy Spirit. All others—well, it's time to break them. You won't believe how free you can be and how good you can feel!

It is very important to note that breaking a soul tie with a person is not the same thing as *rejecting* the person. It is actually the *loving* thing to do. You don't want them obsessing about you, and you don't want to be obsessing about them. You don't want them controlling you, and you don't want to be controlling them. You do not want any further conversations with them when they aren't even there, and you don't want them doing this with you. You certainly don't want their warfare, and they don't want yours.[2]

This simple prayer will help:

> *By the cross of Jesus Christ I now sever all soul ties with* [name them] *in the Name of Jesus Christ. I am crucified to her, and she is crucified to me. I bring the cross of Christ between us, and I bring the love of Christ between us. I send* [name them]*'s spirit back to her body, and I forbid her warfare to transfer to me or to my domain. I command my spirit back into the Spirit of Jesus Christ in my body. I release* [name them] *to you, Jesus. I entrust her to you. Bless her, God! In Jesus's Name. Amen.*

treasure the gift

The only way to have a friend is to be one.
—Ralph Waldo Emerson

The deepest desire of every human being's heart is to be loved. To be loved in the face of our flaws and failings is a taste of heaven. In heaven we will "know even as we are known" (1 Cor. 13:12, author's paraphrase). We will be completely transformed into the image of Christ, beholding him as he truly is, and we will finally and fully be who we truly are. God knows us inside and out. Right now. In heaven we will know him. And we will know others and be known by them perfectly as well. Not only known but enjoyed. Embraced. Understood. Celebrated. Loved. What a thought.

And what an extraordinary gift it is on this side of paradise to be known and enjoyed here. Friendship is meant to offer us that.

I have prayed for friends. I have sought them out and pursued them. At times I have been desperate for them. But the best ones have come to me as a surprise, unexpected answers to prayers I had forgotten I'd prayed. Friends are gifts to us straight from the heart of God to our own, and no one is better at giving perfect gifts than he is.

They come to us all sorts of ways, these treasures. One I met while our children played at a park and I helped her dig through the sand to find her son's precious lost toy. One sat next to me at church one morning, both of us holding our infant sons, reluctant to relinquish them to the nursery. One came to me through an introduction at a party followed by a shy invitation to meet over coffee. And one came through a request for help.

My friend Jill had moved across the country and sent out an email pleading for help to all she knew who remained in the city she had just left. A dear friend of hers, a spiritual mother, was being evicted from her apartment. She was ill, handicapped, poor, helpless—surely she would freeze to death that very night if no one rallied to her aid.

I knew the urgency was not feigned but also not completely true. Still, in this instance, I had the ability to respond. And in coming to the aid of a stranger in need, I received an unlooked-for jewel from God.

That's what women friends are. They are gems to be treasured. Women friends lend each other their clothes, their recipes, their courage, their ideas, their faith, and their hope. Oh, to be loved and seen and encouraged to continue to sing one's song, offer one's true heart! How blessed I am to live surrounded by women of varying ages, backgrounds, and interests who share the same heartbeat of desire for Jesus!

How happy I was the other day to listen to a voice message from a dear one who didn't speak but merely sang to me, "I just called to say I love you...." At the sound of her voice, joyful and whimsical, encouragement lightened my weighed-down heart. Hooray for voice and text messages! Hooray for telephones!

My friend Rosetta was all for hearing about the daily activities of my life. I had called her from a stop light to check in. I was busy inside and out, driving to and fro on a stream of errands. I was tired and not happy about it. I called Rose in the middle of my lists to say hello but also to complain a little. She didn't let me. Not even a little bit. Instead, she spoke words of loving conviction. "How wonderful that you can get out! How great that you have such a full life! Oh, to be able to walk!" Rosetta's life isn't full with running errands or with running of any kind. She couldn't run. She couldn't walk. Living in a wheelchair, Rose didn't get out much. But she had so much life exuding out of her spirit that sometimes, to my embarrassment, I would forget.

Her words, the words of a friend who knew and loved me, reframed my moment and opened my eyes. Friends do that for one another.

Rosetta spent many of her days looking out the window in her tiny apartment, watching the activity of others more physically able. Her little view of the world was a window of grace, and she invited me to see my life through it. In her company my priorities ordered themselves up correctly. She taught me that love sees with a thankful heart. The simple moments that I, too, often take for granted are the very pearls that join together and make a beautiful life, but only when strung together with thankfulness, linked with grace, shared with an open hand.

Last Friday night Rosetta and I enjoyed an unhurried conversation. Both sitting in our respective chairs, we spoke of thoughtful things: hope, suffering, the mysterious ways of our God. She cried in saying good-bye. I didn't know it would be our last. Come Sunday morning, Rosetta was running. She is free and healed and happy and seeing face-to-face the One who has won her heart. I already miss her. I am going to continue to miss her. But only for a little while. And while I do, I pray I continue to see my life through a window of grace and, in loving friendships, invite others to share the view.

9

beauty forged in suffering

It's a good thing to have all the props pulled out from under us occasionally.
It gives us some sense of what is rock under our feet, and what is sand.
—Madeleine L'Engle, *Glimpses of Grace*

My dear friend is too sick to continue with his chemotherapy. He's due for his fifth of six sessions, but his body has yet to recover enough from session four to be able to withstand the rigors of the next treatment. So he waits, knowing what is coming. He waits for his strength to return so it can be assaulted again. Those who have been through the gauntlet of chemotherapy know the pain, the fatigue, the sickness that overtakes the body from the inside. It is close to unbearable to those going through it and arguably worse for the ones who love them. I asked him if it helped knowing what the experience was going to be like or if it made it worse. He answered without hesitation that knowing what was coming made it much, much worse.

Who would be able to go forward into their life if they knew all that was coming? Not me.

Everywhere we look, people are suffering. Even when we look in the mirror. We wake each morning to a new day rife with possibilities, but we have no idea what will come our way. Joy? Sorrow?

Emily Dickenson said, "Into every life a little rain must fall." She failed to mention torrential hail, hurricanes, and floods. What comes into most people's lives is an endless series of severe thunderstorms. The "little rain" threatens to sweep away our capacity to breathe. And God says that he uses all things for our good. Seriously? What good can possibly come from suffering?

the river

The Yampa River flooded its banks in eastern Colorado. A record snowpack in 2011 raised Lake Powell by thirty-one feet, Lake Shasta by seventeen! In Steamboat Springs, Colorado, the Yampa flooded both parks and parking lots. It encroached upon people's lawns and homes. Sandbags were stacked against it. Still it rushed on, brown and churning.

It would subside. But not for a while yet. Not until the snowpack finished melting.

I love the wildness and power of it. I love the beauty of it, the freedom and the there's-no-stopping-me force of it. But my home is not along the Yampa River. I didn't have to sandbag my little domain. I sent up prayers for protection for those who did.

The river will have its way. The snowpack that winter had rivers flooding all over the western states, and in addition to flooding, the result was an abundance of wildflowers beyond reckoning. They were *gorgeous*. Purple larkspur and yellow arrow leaf carpeted the hillsides. A myriad of flowers— red, purple, blue, white, yellow—painted the world with breathtaking beauty.

The price of which was paid in sandbags.

Yes, into every life a little rain must fall. Spring only comes after winter. Tulips will bloom only if they have endured a freeze. Beauty does come from ashes. But at what cost?

The Grand Canyon has been carved by water over years beyond counting into one of the most beautiful displays of nature in the world. My face too is being etched. My soul is being carved. Forces are at work sculpting me—my life, my views, and my beliefs—honing and shaping and changing me. The process is sometimes painful and sometimes unnoticed, but the effect? Oh, for the grace to see the effect as beautiful. To be able to see our lives, our bodies, our faces, our souls sculpted by time, our choices, and the hand of our relentless, fierce, and loving God as beautiful displays.

Rain serves a purpose. Even floodwaters. Even suffering.

finding peace in difficult circumstances

How do you understand your life? Why has it turned out so differently from what you imagined? What do you make of its randomness? The phone rings, and you have no idea what is coming. It could be great news! It could be an old friend getting back in touch! Maybe you won a car! Or it could be something much different.

I went to get a mammogram with one of my girlfriends. She suggested we go together so that we actually *would* go, and then we could celebrate having it over with by going out to lunch. We did. A week later when I next saw her, I asked, "Did you get your clean-bill-of-health letter?" She didn't get that letter. She got a phone call. And another mammogram. And a biopsy. And the battle for her life. I came out as normal, and she came out with stage IV breast cancer. It felt like our two names had been put in a hat, and this time her name was drawn.

In John 16:33 Jesus says, "In this world you will have trouble." Is he not the master of understatement?

Christianity is not a promise to enjoy a life without pain nor to be given a shortcut through it. It is a promise that pain, sorrow, sin—ours and others'—will not swallow us, destroy us, define us, or have the final word. Jesus has won the victory. And in him so have we.

> *I will have nothing to do with a God who cares only occasionally. I need a God who is with us always, everywhere, in the deepest depths as well as the highest heights. It is when things go wrong, when good things do not happen, when our prayers seem to have been lost, that God is most present. We do not need the sheltering wings when things go smoothly. We are closest to God in the darkness, stumbling along blindly.*
> —Madeleine L'Engle, *Two-Part Intervention*

No one gets a pain-free life. I know some women's lives look pretty perfect from a distance, but only from a distance. You get close and you learn the truth. A life without suffering is a fantasy life, and you don't live in a fantasy. No, your life is much more the stuff of fairy tales. Really. There are wicked witches in fairy tales. There are dragons. In fairy tales, big bad wolves devour beloved grandmothers, and little girls wander the woods alone and afraid.

Hard times come to everyone. Our current address is far from Eden. We live in a fallen world with broken people, and we ourselves are not yet all that we are meant to be. Life is difficult on most days, but sometimes it is painful beyond measure.

Peter writes, "Dear friends, do not be surprised at the painful trial you are suffering, as though something strange were happening to you" (1 Pet. 4:12). But we are surprised, aren't we? We wonder, what did we do wrong? Or are we wrong about God? What we believe about God is quickly exposed by pain. What's he like, *really*? Is he mean? Is he harsh? Is he mad at us? Does he not care? Does he not see? Did we fall through the cracks of the universe? The very first thing painful trials try to do is separate us from God. But being separated from God is the worst thing that can happen, much worse than the most excruciating of trials.

When suffering comes, we don't want to jump to conclusions. But it is a good idea to ask God, "What is this? What's going on here?" A terrible flu has swept through our town this season. It hit us hard, but it hit a friend of mine harder. As I talked with her one day, she confessed, "I wish I would learn what God is trying to teach me so I could get over this flu." What was she assuming about God? She was assuming that every sickness was from him. That simply isn't true. We live in a fallen world. The flu goes around. Sickness is not a punishment from God. He is not waiting for her to grasp some deeper truth about herself or to repent of some hidden sin before he heals her. He is not holding out on her (or us) to finally get her act together in order to bless her. He is not a mean God but a loving one filled with grace and mercy. It is his kindness that draws us to repentance, not his cruelty. God will use painful trials, even the flu, to hone us, but he doesn't cause all of them.

Some of my readers will need some help with this because they've been taught a theology that God causes all things. So they have had to swallow hard and accept the view that God caused them to be sexually abused, God caused their mother to die a premature death, God caused their son or daughter to abandon the faith. Oh friends, this is a horrible view of God and a profound *heresy*. Listen:

> When tempted, no one should say, "God is tempting me."
> For God cannot be tempted by evil, nor does he tempt
> anyone; but each person is tempted when they are dragged
> away by their own evil desire and enticed. Then, after desire
> has conceived, it gives birth to sin; and sin, when it is full-
> grown, gives birth to death. (James 1:13–15 NIV 2011)

James makes it clear in this passage that God does not tempt anyone to sin, nor does he go on to cause them to sin. But people are tempted every day; they go on to sin every day. So, then, things happen every single day that God is *not* causing. God does not make anyone sin, but people sin every day, *and those sins have terrible consequences.* This is not God doing these things. Do you see what an important difference it makes?

In his sovereign power God created a world where the choices of angels and human beings matter. We are not puppets on a string. When someone sins, it is not God causing them to sin. That sexual abuse was not arranged by God; he did not cause your brother to be raped any more than he caused those terrorists to bomb the train station.

It is crucial for us to be careful with our *interpretation* of events. We must ask God's help in making sense of it all. But for heaven's sake, don't blame the sin of the world on God. Ever since Adam and Eve sinned, this world has been badly, badly broken. Not only did sin enter in, but the natural world itself spiraled into brokenness. Disease entered in. Maybe you have a terrible flu because someone sneezed on your shopping cart or your child brought it home from school. God did not place those germs on your cart for you to get them.

But yes, God can and does use the suffering of this world to shape us. Maybe you have the flu because you have been living your life at breakneck speed and refusing to rest and take care of your body. Maybe. We need to ask Jesus for his interpretation. Your *interpretation* of the events will shape everything that follows. It will shape your emotions, your perspective, and your decisions. What if you are wrong?

first things first

John and I learned long ago that in cases of suffering, you can have understanding or you can have Jesus. If you insist on understanding, you usually lose both.

When suffering enters into your life, take a deep breath. The very first thing to do is to invite Jesus into it. Pray, *Jesus, catch my heart*. When painful trials come your way, by all means ask God what's up—ask him to interpret it for you. But whether he provides understanding or not, invite Jesus in. Keep inviting Jesus into the pain. Invite Jesus into the places in your heart that are rising to the surface through the suffering, be those painful memories, unbelief, or self-contempt. Pray, *Please come meet me here, Jesus. I need you.*

Let suffering be the door you walk through that draws you to deeper intimacy with Jesus. Suffering can do that, if we let it. And though it would never be the doorway we would choose, it is one we will never regret walking through.

Remember the old bumper sticker "Jesus Is the Answer"? I used to mock that bumper sticker. *What's the question?* I'd think. "How long do you bake a potato?" "Jesus." "Where should I get my car insurance from?" "Jesus." But the older I get, the surer I become that the bumper sticker had it right. Jesus *is* the answer. He is the answer to every substantive question of my heart and need in my soul. And boy, do my needs and questions surface when I am distressed.

"*In all* their *distress he too was* distressed" (Isa. 63:9). We can know that in our distress God too is distressed. Jesus understands heartbreak, betrayal, abandonment, loneliness, sorrow, and pain. He is acquainted with grief. He cares. He cares for you.

God promises, "I will never leave you or forsake you" (Heb. 13:5, author's paraphrase). The original Greek is difficult to translate because of the strong emphasis on *never*—it's a triple negative. God wants you to know that you will never, never, never be abandoned by him. Ever. Never ever. He promises to never leave you or forsake you no matter what you've done or what you are suffering. We hold on to that.

Let me say this again. Let suffering be the door you walk through that draws you to deeper intimacy with Jesus. Let it play its sanctifying role.

Because though God doesn't cause all the trials in our lives, he does use them. He does work all things for our good. He will use pain to expose our false beliefs about our hearts and about his heart. He will use it to prick a place in us that has been wounded here before, to reveal our brokenness so that God can heal it. He will use suffering to reveal Jesus's faithfulness, kindness, and unending love for us.

You see, there is more going on here than meets the eye. There is a battle raging over the human heart. Will we love God and choose to trust the goodness of his heart in the face of the immense brokenness of the world? Will we stand in our belief that God is worthy of our worship and praise in the face of the immense brokenness in our world?

> The Spirit of the Sovereign LORD is on me,
>   because the LORD has anointed me
>   to preach good news to the poor.
> He has sent me to bind up the brokenhearted,
>   to proclaim freedom for the captives
>   and release from darkness for the prisoners,
> to proclaim the year of the LORD's favor
>   and the day of vengeance of our God,
> to comfort all who mourn,
>   and provide for those who grieve in Zion—
> to bestow on them a crown of beauty
>   instead of ashes,
> the oil of gladness
>   instead of mourning,
> and a garment of praise
>   instead of a spirit of despair.
> They will be called oaks of righteousness,

> a planting of the LORD
> for the display of his splendor. (Isa. 61:1–3)

There may not be a more beautiful passage in all of Scripture. If you've read any of my and John's books, you know it is our favorite. Because *this* is what Jesus declared he came to do. He announced that he had come to heal the brokenhearted, to set the captive free. He came to restore us in him and to him. He came to comfort those who grieve, to bestow on them a crown of beauty instead of ashes and a garment of praise instead of a spirit of despair. He says that sorrow may last for the night, but joy comes in the morning. It comes with the morning star. It comes with Jesus. Jesus is the answer. Always.

How do you find peace in the midst of difficult, painful circumstances? Let Peace find you. He's right where you are, right smack dab in the middle of your life.

In the midst of our joy, our busyness, our sorrow, and our suffering, we must turn our gaze on Jesus. Invite Jesus in. Ask him to prove to you once again that he is who he says he is. He says he is our Strength. Our Shield. Our Rock. Our Hiding Place. Our Refuge. Our Deliverer. Our great Comforter, our faithful Companion, and our ever-present Friend. Jesus says he is the mighty God, the Prince of Peace. We can trust him.

Jesus is the only one who can meet the deepest needs of your heart, and he wants you to know how deeply he loves you so badly that he's moved heaven and earth to do it. He is the only one who will never disappoint you, never ever leave you, comfort you intimately, and love you perfectly every single moment of your life. Invite him in.

beauty *will* come

My mother could be a very driven woman; we couldn't walk on the carpet in the living room because we would leave footprints. My mom could be short with me; she could be controlling and demanding; she failed in many ways. Not in every way, not by a long shot, but she did have her rough edges. My mother also loved Jesus. When cancer began to ravage her life when she was seventy-one, a startling transformation began to take place. My mother softened; she became gentler than she was before—or she became gentle more often. She loosened her grasp on control; it just didn't matter. She lost her edge to demand or criticize. She said "I love you" more than she ever had. The beauty that was always there began to come forth in truly amazing ways. Our last four months together were the best months of love and relationship we ever shared.

My mother suffered intensely during the last months of her life. She had suffered much in the long years prior to them as well. But in those final months, she leaned into God and came to know his love in a way that filled her heart with peace, rest, and joy. Unable to swallow anything, my mom received nourishment via a feeding tube. A tiny sip of water was impossible for her to take down. She hoped that when she crossed over from life to Life, Jesus would be waiting for her with a large, cold glass of water.

My mom kept a diary all her life. Not journals, diaries; little entries of how she spent her days. A few months after she died, I was reading through her diary from her last year of life when a note in her precious handwriting fell out. This is what it said:

> I wish to thank the beautiful priests and parishioners at St. Edwards Church and San Felipe de Jesus for their prayers during my illness. I had an unexpected diagnosis, and it has been the most awesome, rewarding, and glorious time God has ever given to me. I thank God the Father, Son, and Holy Spirit from the depth of my soul. ~ Mary Jane Morris

My mother actually gave thanks in her suffering—not *for* the suffering, but for what it did in her life. It opened her up to relationship; it caused her to see the value of love over clean carpets and a neat kitchen; it enabled her to offer love and receive love. And though her battle with cancer ended up costing her life, what she gained through the pain she named "the most awesome, rewarding, and glorious time God has ever given me."

And she's drinking Living Water now!

Our dear friend's brother, Lance, just went to heaven. He was thirty years old and had spent the last eighteen months of his life in a courageous battle against brain cancer. Days before he died, his grieving mother wrote this: "Father Richard has helped me to understand if we don't let pain transform us, we will surely transmit it.... Reflect on this.... May all of our sorrow and loss be turned into compassion." The pain and sorrow in our lives is used by our loving God to transform us. Let it do its powerful sanctifying work.

I am surrounded by people who are surrendering their lives to Jesus in deeper ways. They may not understand why things have happened as they have, but they are trusting God that no matter what, he is good. Our friend Scott has grown to know and trust God profoundly. He sent us a little note on the twenty-eighth anniversary of his fall from a ladder that left him paralyzed from the waist down. Scott and his wife know God in a way few of us do. He simply wrote, "No regrets." The note brought John and me to tears.

God didn't give my mom cancer any more than he caused Scott to fall. He didn't cause it. But he will use it. He will use it to reveal to us who he really is in the face of tragedy and anguish. He will use it to reveal to us who we really are. Jesus wants you to know who you are. He wants us to see ourselves as our Father sees us. The most important mirror for us to look in is our reflection in his eyes.

I would like to become a woman who is as desperate for God in my joy as I am in my sorrow. That has not happened yet. Nothing brings my heart to fully run after God like being in a season of grief. It may be grief over the way I have failed my sons or my husband. It may be sorrow over a revelation of how my selfishness has hurt my friends. It may be pain over the suffering that one I love is experiencing. But nothing causes me to seek God like pain.

thank you

I don't pretend that suffering always has a good effect on us. I've known women made hard, angry, and jealous by their suffering. They envied those who did not seem to be suffering as they were; they even went so far as to wish suffering upon them so that "they would know what it's like." This is tragedy; this is ugly. We never, ever want to wish suffering upon another person.

How do we allow suffering to do a holy work in us, and not let it make us envious, hard, angry women?

First, I think we need to be honest about what we *have* done with our suffering. What have we allowed it to do to our hearts? Have we become more fearful? Controlling? Has resentment toward God or others entered in? Let us quickly bring that to Jesus, for this is cancer of the soul, and it ravages what God means to make lovely. We renounce our anger or envy, our controlling or bitterness. We bring it quickly under the blood of Jesus and ask him to remove it all from our heart and soul.

We also need his healing love. We ask him to do in us the very thing he promised in Isaiah 61:

> *Jesus, heal my broken heart, release me from all darkness.*
> *Comfort me in my suffering. Cleanse me from all evil that has*
> *gotten in or taken root in the places of my sorrow. Comfort*
> *me. Give me a crown of beauty instead of ashes; make me*

beautiful here, Lord, in this. Give me the oil of gladness instead of mourning; lift my grief and sorrow and give me the oil of your gladness; give me a garment of praise instead of a spirit of despair. Rescue me.

I think we can hasten this process of healing. I think it begins with that last phrase about praise instead of despair. Nothing—nothing—undoes the harmful effects of suffering as our choice to begin to love and worship Jesus in the midst of it.

I was talking with a friend—both her wrists were in casts from carpal-tunnel syndrome, her fibromyalgia was flaring up and making any movement painful, and her autistic daughter had just been sent home from school again for threatening a classmate. My friend loves God and believes his Word, so she thinks that though she doesn't understand it, she must give thanks to God for it. Really? Thank you for the illness and the emotional devastation?

No.

The Scriptures are not telling us to give thanks to God *for* every wicked, evil, hard, painful, excruciating, grief-filled thing that happens in our or others' lives. That is not what it means. That would be calling evil good. And we are also told by Scripture never ever to do that. No, my sister, what the Scripture says is this: "Rejoice always, pray continually, give thanks in all circumstances; for this is God's will for you in Christ Jesus" (1 Thess. 5:16–18 NIV 2011). Give thanks to God *in* every situation, not *for* every situation.

By loving Jesus in our pain, we allow him *into* our pain.

Being thankful opens up windows in the spiritual realm for the presence of God to fill our lives, our thoughts, our understanding, and our perspective. It opens up the doors to the blessings that God wants to pour into our lives. We will come to a place of increasing gratefulness for the story of our lives, both the joyful times and the excruciating seasons. The golden moments that we cherish forever and the awful moments we can't seem to forget. We are on our way to the place of being able to exalt God over all of it. Yes, all of it.

In *Jesus Calling*, Sarah Young wrote,

> Thankfulness is not some sort of magic formula; it is the language of Love, which enables you to communicate intimately with Me. A thankful mind-set does not entail a denial of reality with its plethora of problems. Instead, it *rejoices in Me, your Savior*, in the midst of trials and tribulations. *I am your refuge and strength, an ever present and well proved help in trouble.*[1]

When Jesus rose from the dead and appeared to his disciples, Thomas was not present. So Jesus came back to them again, when Thomas was also in their midst. Do you recall how Jesus proved that he was real, and risen, and still the same Jesus they had always known and loved? He told Thomas, "Put your hands in my scars." Jesus still had his scars then, and he still has them today. They are Jesus's glory. They are what we most worship him for. Glorified Jesus still has his scars, and when we reach glory, so will we. But they will be beautiful, like his.

The story of my life and the struggles I have lived with—make that "live with"—have helped to shape me into the woman I am today and the woman I am becoming. My scars, my struggles, my failures, my joys, my private lonely agonies have been forging my soul into something beautiful. Eternal. Good. Yours have too.

Now, we can fight that process—or we can yield to it. My dear mother had her rough edges; you have yours; I have mine. We can choose to let suffering soften us or harden us. We can choose whether we will allow it to make us more compassionate or let our hearts become jealous of others. We can choose whether we will love Jesus in it or resent him for it. Only one set of choices will make us more beautiful.

The pain we experience, the sorrow and the agony, serve a purpose. God *is* working all things together for our good. He is etching a masterpiece of stunning design. The beauty being forged in us through the transforming work of suffering is one that will leave us breathless, stunned, and forever thankful. And the crowning glory will be that because of the pain we have endured, we have come to know Jesus in a way that causes us to treasure the trial as one of God's greatest gifts to us. Amazing.

10

stumbling into freedom

*It is for freedom that Christ has set us free. Stand firm, then, and
do not let yourselves be burdened again by a yoke of slavery.*
—Paul, Galatians 5:1

John and I went to the zoo on Saturday. I loved seeing live-and-in-person
lions, snow leopards, giraffes, elephants, gorillas, piranhas, and glow-in-the-
dark tree frogs. There was an amazing section of oriental birds decorated
more intricately than geishas. I've never seen anything like them before.
There were flamingos, California condors, and two bald eagles enclosed in
a habitat with high nets. There was a turtle that lives at the bottom of lakes
that was the ugliest thing I have ever seen. Crazy. Wonderful.

Later that same day, we went for a hike in the hills. It was a glorious
sunny day with a strong breeze blowing. Coming back down, we stopped
at the cry of a hawk and looked up to see three of them: soaring, diving
so fast, then up, up, up. Chasing each other, then hovering and still—they
flew with the aerial gymnastics of angels.

They were awesome. They were *free*.

I felt bad for the wild birds I had just seen in captivity. I understand zoos, I am not anti-zoo, but living in cages is not what those birds were created for. They are not living their best life now! At the zoo it had been wonderful to see bald eagles up so close. How huge they are! But I've seen bald eagles eating fish on the banks of the Snake River. I've seen them looking out over their domain from the protected heights of a stately pine, and I've seen them battling golden eagles over their nests.

Freedom is better than captivity.

So why in heaven's name would anyone choose captivity? Why do we live so long in the bondage we find ourselves in? There's a passage in Isaiah that we shine up on the screens at the women's retreats we hold:

> Shake off your dust;
>   rise up, sit enthroned, Jerusalem.
> Free yourself from the chains on your neck,
>   Daughter Zion, now a captive. (52:2 NIV 2011)

Free yourself? Isn't it Jesus who sets us free? Indeed he does; he already has in ways that will take your breath away. But we have a part to play. God calls us to rise up, shake the dust off, sit enthroned. We have a part to play in our freedom.

Why does anyone choose captivity? Well, captives do get fed. On a regular basis. They're safe in their cages, their cells, their prisons. In the movie *The Shawshank Redemption*, longtime prisoner and now ringleader Red has been incarcerated for decades. He confesses, "These walls are funny. First you hate 'em, then you get used to 'em. Enough time passes, you get so you depend on them."[1]

Prisons can be safe and comfortable. They can become a known life, a familiar way. Resignation is safe; dreaming is dangerous. Letting someone else control your life is easier than rising up to deny them that control; the relationship will never be the same. Living under shame can feel far easier than fighting for your own dignity. The known is always more comfortable and less risky than the unknown. After a while, those animals in the zoo forget they were even made for the open skies, the wild savannahs. This is a horrible place to come to. Not a one of us was created to live in captivity.

By the way, there can be many zookeepers in our lives. We can chain ourselves through years of bad habits, bad mental patterns, chosen idolatries that become our addictions. Other people can chain us through their expectations and demands. Many people have a picture in their minds of who we ought to be and how we should be living. Cultures can chain us; religions can chain us. And of course behind it all we have an Enemy who loves nothing more than to keep us in prison. We will have to choose freedom and fight for our freedom as the Scripture urges.

Let me ask you, dear one: what would you *love* to be free from? Is it sorrow? Regret? Resentment, addiction, shame, fear, worry, doubts?

What would you *love* to be free to do? Live your life? Follow your dreams? Love with abandon? Worship God? *Experience* Jesus—follow him, know him, *believe* him?

This is all a part of our becoming. As we become the woman God always meant us to be, we are able to step into more and more freedom. And as we step more and more into freedom, we become the woman we were meant to be. It can happen; it can be yours.

So why would captive Daughter Zion have to be told to free herself from the chains around her neck? We choose captivity over freedom because we are afraid of the price.

When Sabatina James, an eighteen-year-old Pakistani woman, rejected the arranged marriage her parents had made for her, her life became a living hell. After she refused to live within the confines of her family's cultural parameters, her mother began to call her cruel names and beat her while alone or even in larger family gatherings. When the violence escalated and her parents threatened to murder her, she ran away. (The UN estimates that five thousand girls are murdered around the world every year by their parents for acting in ways they feel shame the family.) Living in Germany now, Sabatina said, "I rarely go out alone. I often wonder if someone is lurking around the corner. I have always loved my freedom—but I have paid a high price."[2]

Yes, freedom can be costly. We know that. But sister, captivity is always more costly. You pay too high a price to stay in chains. Freedom is what you are made for; freedom is *good*.

we were meant to be free

> For it is written that Abraham had two sons, one by the slave woman and the other by the free woman. His son by the slave woman was born in the ordinary way; but his son by the free woman was born as the result of a promise. (Gal. 4:22–23)

Okay, I'll confess I never liked the story of Hagar and Sarah. (You'll find it in the Old Testament, tucked between the Tower of Babel and the destruction of Sodom and Gomorrah.) I've always felt bad for Hagar. I mean, she was Sarah's slave. She didn't have a choice of whether to obey or not. It was Sarah—who was barren and mighty bitter about it—who cooked up the plan to have her husband, Abraham, sleep with Hagar in the hope that perhaps she could bear him a son. It's a messy story.

But in the New Testament we are urged to read the story figuratively, as a kind of parable, a spiritual picture:

> These things may be taken figuratively, for the women represent two covenants. One covenant is from Mount

> Sinai and bears children who are to be slaves: This is
> Hagar. Now Hagar stands for Mount Sinai in Arabia and
> corresponds to the present city of Jerusalem, because she
> is in slavery with her children. But the Jerusalem that is
> above is free, and she is our mother. (Gal. 4:24–26)

Hagar is the bondswoman, and she represents bondage. Her son, Ishmael, represents the *fruit* that comes from being in bondage. By staying in relationship with Hagar and Ishmael and keeping them close, Sarah and Abraham were preventing Isaac from being able to receive his full God-given inheritance as a son. When Isaac was weaned, his father Abraham threw him a big party to celebrate (Gen. 21). Hagar was there and so was Ishmael. And they were jealous. Ishmael mocked Isaac just like the fruit of bondage in our life mocks us—be that the scale or the bank account or the failures we relive as we lie awake at night.

Genesis tells us that Hagar *despised* Sarah. The word used in Genesis means cursed. She and her son hated and mocked Isaac as well. They cursed him. They wanted the inheritance from Abraham for themselves. They did not want it to go to the one God had given it to.

> Now you, brothers and sisters, like Isaac, are children of
> promise. At that time the son born according to the flesh
> persecuted the son born by the power of the Spirit. It is
> the same now. But what does Scripture say? "Get rid of
> the slave woman and her son, for the slave woman's son
> will never share in the inheritance with the free woman's
> son." (Gal. 4:28–30 NIV 2011)

Sarah dealt harshly with them. "Get rid of that slave woman and her son," she told Abraham (Gen. 21:10). Abraham felt bad about that. He went to his tent and asked God what to do, and God told him, "Do what Sarah said. Make them leave" (v. 12, author's paraphrase). So he did, and they left. (And by the way, God took great care of Hagar and Ishmael. He dealt kindly with them.) This story is actually about our need as believers to cast out any and all bondage from our life. And after we have done so, not to let ourselves be burdened again by a yoke of slavery. It is about casting out the fruit of that bondage as well.

> It is for freedom that Christ has set us free. Stand firm, then, and do not let yourselves be burdened again by a yoke of slavery. (Gal. 5:1)

God has given each of us an inheritance in Christ. Jesus came that we might have life and life to the full. When we get into relationships with people or institutions or into patterns of behavior or addictions that are not God's highest for us, they get in the way of our being able to receive what God has for us. We are to deal strongly with areas of bondage in our life. We are not to make excuses for them but cast them out. Make them leave. We say no to bondage, no to mocking spirits, no to accusing spirits. We say no—fiercely and firmly to any accusation that we are (fill in the blank—what are you accused of being?) unloving, disqualified, stuck, mean, unforgiving, lacking in faith, lacking in beauty, or lacking—period. And we say yes to God and yes to what he has spoken over our life. Yes to his promises.

Like Isaac, you have a God-given inheritance. You have a destiny. You are a daughter. You are also a bride. You are a coheir with Christ. Your inheritance in Christ is freedom and life and joy and every good gift. Your inheritance is victory and a heart that is not striving or filled with fear but at rest. It's holiness and happiness and peace. Your inheritance includes having peace in your soul no matter what is going on in your life. As we walk toward our freedom, we walk toward who we are becoming.

It begins with an internal choice.

choosing to be free inside

Many years ago John and I were members of a wonderful church in Southern California. A young man also attended there who had an amazing spirit and an even more amazing testimony. "Daniel" was from Uganda; he had lived there under the brutal reign of Idi Amin. He had been in prison there, beaten, and tortured—and he had the scars to show for it. He had been imprisoned because he was a Christian.

Many of his days were spent being beaten. During one of his trials, he was hung from his feet and beaten over a period of days. The guard's job—his *job*—was to whip Daniel. After several days of this, after the ritual torture, as his guard was preparing to leave, Daniel said to the guard, "Have a nice evening."

Seriously. He said that. Daniel blessed him. By the grace of Jesus Christ living in his heart, he was able to forgive his oppressors and in that forgiveness rise above the bondage they wanted over his life—the bondage of his heart, mind, and spirit.

"Have a nice evening." My goodness. Which of these two men was truly free?

The guard was undone and incredulously asked, "How can you say that to me? How can you say that?" Daniel told him how. He told him about Jesus, about the price Jesus had paid to win his heart, about the freedom he knew in Christ. He told him about being forgiven and accepted and loved perfectly. And a few days later, that guard helped Daniel to escape. But first he took him home to feed him and have him share the gospel with his family.

Have a nice evening?!?!?!

We can be so free. It all begins here—with an internal choice to let Christ so invade our hearts that we cannot be held to any sort of bondage internally. We choose to love, to forgive; we choose not to fear; we choose life.

Most of us are probably still laboring under the impression that freedom comes first in our circumstances, and then we can experience love, joy, peace, patience, and all the other wonderful fruit of the Spirit. Not so. God usually begins first with the transformation of our attitudes; then he can change our circumstances.

Did you know that you have been set free from sin? Did you know that you now have a good heart? It's true. It happened through the coming of Jesus Christ for you:

> Could it be any clearer? Our old way of life was nailed to the Cross with Christ, a decisive end to that sin-miserable life—no longer at sin's every beck and call! … From now on, think of it this way: Sin speaks a dead language that means nothing to you; God speaks your mother tongue, and you hang on every word. You are dead to sin and alive to God. That's what Jesus did.…
>
> A new power is in operation. The Spirit of life in Christ, like a strong wind, has magnificently cleared the air, freeing you from a fated lifetime of brutal tyranny at the hands of sin and death. (Rom. 6:6, 11; 8:2 MSG)

> I will give you a new heart and put a new spirit in you; I will remove from you your heart of stone and give you a heart of flesh. And I will put my Spirit in you and move you to follow my decrees and be careful to keep my laws. (Ezek. 36:26–27)

He purified their hearts by faith. (Acts 15:9)

We have been given the greatest freedom of all: freedom of heart, freedom from sin, a freedom that enables us to live and love as Jesus did. Let me show you how this works in an area many, many women struggle with.

judge not lest ye be judged

In chapter 3 I talked about how mean women can sometimes be. Girls can be catty, vicious. We cut with our words and even with a look. I think it all comes back to our vulnerability, that glorious vulnerability God gave us when he created us feminine. It also flows out of our relational gifting; God made us masters of relationship. But when fear and insecurity seize upon our vulnerability, we become self-protective. We look for ways to feel better about ourselves, and one of our choicest ways is to bring others down. If we are insecure in ourselves or our life choices, then people who make choices different from ours can feel threatening. We judge.

"She's breastfeeding on demand. She's breastfeeding on a schedule. She isn't breastfeeding. Her children are going to public school. Her children are homeschooled. She's going back to work. She isn't working. Their family is so busy they never have time to sit down to dinner together. They eat only organic food. They eat only processed food. If she exercised more often she wouldn't have those extra ten pounds. She talks too much and laughs too loud. She never speaks. These people are doing it *wrong*!"

Judgments are dangerous; judgments are like curses. They release the hatred of the Enemy upon those we have judged. When Christians pray with a spirit of judgment, it is not a prayer, it is a curse. Christian curses happen when we pray wanting vengeance, when we pray with a spirit of hatred, judgment, anger, or revenge. Prayers like "Get him, God," "Teach him a lesson," "Rebuke him, God" have the same energy as witchcraft.

Actually, they are witchcraft, and they hurt people. They damage them spiritually and physically. They damage us as well. Judgments also backfire; they open the door for judgment to come back upon us.

In Matthew 7:1–2 Jesus says, "Do not judge, or you too will be judged. For in the same way you judge others, you will be judged, and with the measure you use, it will be measured to you."

When we judge others with a sense of righteous indignation—when we enjoy it, feel justified in it—we are opening the door for judgments and curses to come into our lives. When I say "judging," I'm not talking about the wisdom of discernment between evil and good. I'm talking about cursing others.

Some dear friends are the only Christians in their extended family. It is a close family system (some might say too close), and the rule is that all members are always present for any holiday. (This is a good example of a family acting as a zookeeper, creating a bondage for its members.) As our friends have grown in Christ they have chosen not to attend every family obligation. This has brought a lot of judgment on them. They experience that judgment as a real spiritual oppression; of course, it is. It is sin, and it is permission for the Enemy to oppress.

The problem is this: our friends are judging back. In their hearts and words, they continually judge their family for judging them! (It gets pretty twisted.) And they can't get free of the relational bondage or especially the spiritual cursing of those judgments until they first repent of their judging.

And I'm wondering, how many relationships between women are ensnared in the same dynamic?

We can be free from judgments, or at least more free—free from judging others and free from the effect of others judging us.

God says to bless those who are cursing us. In his wild, free, and amazing love, he instructs us to pray blessing over people—pray blessing over people who have hurt you, judged you, maligned you, rejected you, or simply misunderstood you, or who have done that to someone you love very much. Pray blessing on them. The truth is that's what you want. Pray more of Jesus for people! Because when they become blessed and happy and close to Jesus, they won't be hating on you and those you care for anymore! Also, you will receive blessing instead of cursing as well.

The spiritual principle here is you reap what you sow. Bless. Bless. Bless. "Shower people with your favor, God, with your love, with your Presence!"

We want to be free of judgment, and because of Jesus we can be free. We can be free from:

> Bondage
> Sin
> The fear of man
> Shame
> Regret
> Rage
> Disappointment
> Addiction
> Fear
> You name it.

We are no longer captives to sin. We are no longer slaves to the Enemy, to the world, or to our own flesh. We have been released. We are not only free from, we are free to! We are free to be transformed into the very image of Christ. We are free to love in the face of hatred. Free to become the fullest expression of our unique selves. Free to offer to others the beauty that God planted in us when he first dreamed of us. We are free to:

> Be happy
> Be glorious

Succeed

Love

Live

Forgive

Not be bound by any chains

Because of what Jesus has done for us! We have been ransomed, paid for, saved, and freed to be who we really are and do what we are meant to do.

You know that catchy saying, "Dance as though no one is watching you. Love as though you have never been hurt. Sing as though no one can hear you. Live as though heaven is on earth"? I've never liked that. I've thought, how can anyone be free to love like they've never been hurt? How can we do that when we have been hurt and hurt badly?

How can we be free to dance like no one is watching? Unless you are home alone with the curtains drawn, people are probably watching. How do we live in freedom? We live in freedom when we come to believe, know, receive, and embrace the boundless love of God for us—when we are captured by his goodness, his faithfulness, his honor, his sacrifice, his heart that yearns for us. Then we can dance for an audience of One. Because we are so completely loved. We are safe and secure in the love of God. Every moment of our lives.

This brings us another startling freedom: we are free to fail. Let me say that again. We are free to fail. Because of Jesus, we can be free from the cages of other people's expectations, demands, yokes, and judgments—even our own.

This isn't about getting it perfect, dear one. We are loved, forgiven, embraced; we live under grace, not under judgment. It sets us free from perfectionism, which is a terrible prison. It sets us free even to fail.

My emotions waver. My physical strength and spiritual life have variables. One day I am strong in Christ, believing everything God says, and on another day I am not so strong. That's okay. I will never be free from needing God, and neither will you. He alone is perfect, valiant, complete. And in him, so are we. But only *in him*.

> Now the Lord is the Spirit, and where the Spirit of the Lord is, there is freedom. And we all, who with unveiled faces contemplate the Lord's glory, are being transformed into his image with ever increasing glory, which comes from the Lord, who is the Spirit. (2 Cor. 3:17–18 NIV 2011)

freedom from spiritual bondage

The other night I was lying on the floor with worship music playing. But I wasn't lying on the floor worshipping. I was wondering. The day had not been a great one. I was exhausted from travel and too many conversations and thought the answer to my physical and emotional state would be found in pizza and chocolate ice cream. I chose to spend the entire day in old patterns of living that have never proven helpful. Lying on the floor, listening to the music, I asked God, "Do you really love me now? Here? How can you possibly love me in this low place?"

But I knew he did. Jesus died on the cross for all of my sins, even the ones I have committed over and over and over again. There was a battle going on for my freedom that day. And it was raging where it almost always rages: over what I would choose to believe.

It wouldn't be right for me to talk about our freedom in Christ without addressing spiritual warfare at least a little bit. In *Waking the Dead*, my husband, John, wrote, "You won't understand your life, you won't see clearly what has happened to you or how to live forward from here, unless you see it as *battle*. A war against your heart."[3] Jesus has won our freedom in a spiritual showdown with Satan. But our Enemy still refuses to go down without a fight. He knows he cannot take down Jesus, the Victorious One. But he can still wound his heart by wounding ours. Jesus has won our freedom. But we need to receive it, claim it, and stand in it. That is our good fight of faith: believing God is who he says he is and believing we are who he says we are in the face of evidence surrounding us that screams the opposite.

In order for us to live in freedom and become the women we are to become, we need to receive God's love even in our lowest places.

Spiritual warfare is designed to separate you from the love of God. Its goal is to keep you from living in the freedom that Jesus has purchased for you. Satan whispers to us when we have failed or sinned or are feeling horrid that we are nothing and no one. He is a liar. And our fight for our freedom involves exposing him for who he is even when the lies feel completely true. The battle is waged and won in our thought life: in our minds and in our *hearts*.

So what are you thinking? (Yeah, right now.) Descartes famously wrote, "I think, therefore I am." I would add a fill-in-the-blank in each phrase. I think I am _____, therefore I am _____. I think I am kind, there-fore I am kind. I think I am chosen, therefore I am chosen. I think I am becoming more loving, therefore I am becoming more loving. I think I am forever bound to sin, therefore I am forever bound to sin. What we think about ourselves, others, or a circumstance informs how we perceive it, which informs the way we experience it. Our thoughts play out in our lives.

> We demolish arguments and every pretension that sets itself
> up against the knowledge of God, and we take captive every
> thought to make it obedient to Christ. (2 Cor. 10:5)

What do you think about God? What do you think about yourself? Who are you? What do you think life is about? What do you think is true? Because what you think informs your reality and has a direct effect on how you live your life. What we focus on, we move toward. What we look at, esteem, molds us in its direction. What we think is true plays out in our moment-by-moment existence. What are you thinking?

Surely you desire truth in the inner parts. (Ps. 51:6)

Thy word is truth. (John 17:17 KJV)

But when he, the Spirit of truth, comes, he will guide you into all truth. (John 16:13)

In order to recognize a lie, we need to know the truth. Experts in counterfeit money don't spend their time studying counterfeits. They study the real currency. In the same way, to engage in the spiritual battle raging around us, we don't shift our focus to lies or to the Devil. We focus on Jesus. We marinate in the truth of who God is and who he says we are. Then and only then will we be able to quickly recognize a lie. And though there are some areas of bondage in our lives where truth is not going to be enough to set us completely free, we will never get any freedom at all without it.

Remember when Jesus was in the wilderness and the Devil came to tempt him? Jesus didn't reason with the Enemy. He didn't engage with him in a dialogue; he simply refuted him with the truth. "Then you will know the truth, and the truth will set you free" (John 8:32).

So, Spiritual Warfare Level One: you have an Enemy. You are hated. Evil exists. Satan exists. Foul spirits exist. Peter writes, "Be alert and of sober mind. Your enemy the devil prowls around like a roaring lion looking for someone to devour" (1 Pet. 5:8 NIV 2011). Devour, not tempt. Devour as in shred, maul, kill, destroy. James commands,

"Submit yourselves, then, to God. Resist the devil, and he will flee from you" (James 4:7).

If we do not submit to God, the Devil will not flee. If we do not resist the Devil, he will not flee. There is no reason to fear or strive. But we do need to submit to God and resist the Devil. We enforce the freedom Jesus has won for us by believing and agreeing with the truth. This is a big, big part of "shake off your dust; rise up, sit enthroned, Jerusalem. Free yourself from the chains on your neck, Daughter Zion, now a captive" (Isa. 52:2 NIV 2011). Time to rise up, girl.[4]

Spiritual laws need to be enforced just like traffic laws. When you are dealing with fallen angels, think Somali pirates, sex traffickers, the Mafia, law breakers who hate authority, rebel against it, and breathe death and destruction. Demons don't stop harassing you if you don't force them to stop harassing you.

We can no longer afford to let our thoughts run wild. What we think on *matters*. We have to make it a practice to regularly check in on our hearts, our thoughts. What are we believing? What agreements are we making? Why? When we become aware that our thoughts are not aligned with the Word of God, we repent and elevate our thoughts to agree with God. When we become aware of agreements we are making with the Enemy, like, "Life is hard, then you die," or "I will never change," we break those agreements. Out loud. As in:

> *I renounce this lie. I break every agreement I have been making with my Enemy. I renounce the agreement that [I am overwhelmed; I'll never get free; I hate so-and-so; I am stupid, ugly, fat, depressed—name it, and break with it]. I renounce this in the Name of Jesus Christ my Lord.*

Regardless of how you feel.

what is true?

The one who is in you is greater than the one who is in the world. (1 John 4:4)

For he has rescued us from the dominion of darkness and brought us into the kingdom of the Son he loves, in whom we have redemption, the forgiveness of sins. (Col. 1:13–14)

And having disarmed the powers and authorities [spiritual powers and spiritual authorities], he made a public spectacle of them, triumphing over them by the cross. (Col. 2:15)

All authority in heaven and earth has been given to me. (Matt. 28:18)

But because of his great love for us, God, who is rich in mercy, made us alive with Christ even when we were dead in transgressions—it is by grace you have been saved. And God raised us up with Christ and seated us with him in the heavenly realms in Christ Jesus. (Eph. 2:4–6)

I have given you authority to trample on snakes and scorpions and to overcome all the power of the enemy; nothing will harm you. However, do not rejoice that the spirits submit to you, but rejoice that your names are written in heaven. (Luke 10:19–20)

Daughter of Zion—daughter of the true King—you rise up and sit enthroned when you take your position in Christ and command the Enemy to leave.

The Enemy has been disarmed by the cross of Jesus Christ. When we engage in spiritual warfare *we are enforcing* what has already been accomplished. That's how you free yourself from the chains around your neck!

A basic tool for recognizing if you are under spiritual attack or dealing with foul spirits is to judge the fruit: "By their fruit you will recognize them" (Matt. 7:16). Is misunderstanding coming against your friendships? Pray against that. *I bring the cross and blood of Jesus Christ against all misunderstanding and command it bound to his throne—by his authority and in his Name.* Are you feeling fear? Discouragement? Self-hatred? The fruit of all that is pretty obvious—it is foul, dark, and from hell. Resist it in the Name of Jesus.

I am not being simplistic. I understand that often many other issues are involved: our brokenness, our sin, our history. Sometimes there's a reason we struggle with certain things. That's why James says we should first submit to God, then resist the Devil.

For instance, say you keep getting hit hard with a spirit of resentment. Commanding it to leave will not make it go away if you are entertaining resentment in your heart and engaging it in your imagination. If you've opened the door to it by agreeing with it in your thoughts. First you have to repent of resentment toward others, yourself, and God. Repent. You seek the healing of Jesus in the wounds that allow resentment to come. You choose to love Christ right here, in this very place. This is how you submit to God. *Then* you will have the authority to command it to leave because you've withdrawn the welcome mat.

Familiar spirits are often hard to recognize because they are historic things you have struggled with. For me it would be depression. For many women, it is death. (By the way, daydreaming about your memorial service is not a good idea, and I know I'm not the only woman who has done that. Imagining what people will say, how they'll feel—bad idea. If we are longing for relief from the sorrow of life or our failures through death, we are coming into an agreement with death. Jesus wants life for us. Always. Jesus is Life.

In those moments, invite Jesus into your need and your sorrow.) We need to break every agreement we have made with Satan. With discouragement. Defeat. Despair. Loneliness. Rage. Self-hatred.

Break agreements with it. Even if it feels true. *Especially* if it feels true! Repent of entertaining it, making room for it. Then send it to Jesus. I like to send foul spirits to the throne of Christ for him to decide what to do with them. I don't just want to cast them out of my room, or my house, so they can go on to whomever they desire next. A lot of times, if it's coming against you, it's coming against the others around you as well. Send it to Jesus; forbid its return.

Let's say you walk into a room and are suddenly hit with a wave of fear. Or perhaps you go to bed at night and BOOM, you start worrying about the future, your children, you name it. Fear. There's a mighty strong chance this isn't just you. The Enemy may well be present in the form of a spirit of fear. When that happens to me, here is how I pray:

> *I bring the cross and blood of Jesus Christ against all fear, and in the Name of Jesus Christ and by his authority I command every spirit of fear to leave me now; I send you bound to the throne of Jesus Christ. Go. Now. In Jesus's Name.*

It's good to name the specific spirit you are coming under. It doesn't give it more power; rather it's like opening the door into the cellar and letting the light in. It removes the power. You become aware that you aren't overwhelmed, or full of fear or shame. You aren't intimidated. You don't want to die. No, that's coming from a foul spirit. Rebuke it. Out loud. In the Name of Jesus Christ.

We'd better close this chapter with prayer:

> *Praise you, Jesus. Thank you for all you have accomplished for us. We love you. We worship you. You are the King of*

Kings and Lord of Lords, and your Name is above every other name that can be given in this age or in the age to come. We come under your authority now. We receive all the work that you accomplished for us in your cross and death, in your resurrection, and in your ascension. We take our place in your authority now, and in your Name, Jesus, we come against every foul spirit that has been harassing us. We bring the cross and blood of Jesus Christ against every foul spirit of [what has been attacking you? Hatred, rage, intimidation, shame, accusation, judgment, offense, misunderstanding, fear, panic, dread, hopelessness, despair?] *We bring your blood and cross against these foul spirits. In the Name of Jesus Christ and by his authority we command every foul spirit bound to the throne of Jesus Christ for judgment. We break every agreement we have made with the Enemy, and we renounce them now. We make our agreement with the Truth.*

Father, please send your angels to enforce this command. Thank you, God. Praise you. We worship you, Jesus. We long to be free, to know you and to love you more deeply and truly. You are worthy. Please remove everything that separates us from knowing you as you truly are and keeps us from living in the freedom that you have purchased for us. In Jesus's Mighty Name.

God has done everything, won everything, and given us everything we need to live in freedom. We are meant to walk in it, more and more. We won't walk gracefully into it all the time. But by the grace of God, and with his help, we can stumble into it. One thought at a time. One day at a time.

11

becoming a woman of faith

Crying is all right in its way while it lasts. But you have to stop
sooner or later, and then you still have to decide what to do.
When Jill stopped, she found she was dreadfully thirsty. She had
been lying face downward, and now she sat up. The birds had
ceased singing and there was perfect silence except for one small,
persistent sound, which seemed to come from a good distance away.
She listened carefully, and felt almost sure it was the sound of
running water.... Her thirst was very bad now, and she plucked
up her courage to go and look for that running water....

She came to an open glade and saw the stream, bright as glass,
running across the turf a stone's throw away from her. But although
the sight of the water made her feel ten times thirstier than before,
she didn't rush forward and drink. She stood as still as if she had
been turned to stone, with her mouth wide open. And she had a
very good reason; just on this side of the stream lay the lion.
—C. S. Lewis, *The Silver Chair*

My mother thought I drank too much water. My husband worries that it may not be good for me to drink as much water as I do. I can put down multiple liters a day. I'm not prediabetic, and I have no health issues of major concern; I am simply *thirsty*. Studies show that when a person finally becomes aware of their physical thirst, they are already dehydrated. We are all thirstier than we realize.

We are spiritually thirsty too. We are women of various ages and needs, but like Jill in C. S. Lewis's *The Silver Chair*, we have heard the alluring sound of flowing, life-giving water and have come to the river. We are thirsty women, and that is a very good thing. It may not be *comfortable*, but it is good. If you aren't aware of your hunger, you're not very motivated to go to the banqueting table. If you aren't aware of your thirst, you don't seek something to drink.

There on Aslan's mountain, Jill stood frozen a long time looking at the water and the lion.

> How long this lasted, she could not be sure; it seemed like hours. And the thirst became so bad that she almost felt she would not mind being eaten by a lion if only she could be sure of getting a mouthful of water first.[1]

Finally the lion spoke.

> "If you're thirsty, you may drink."[2]

In our world, we are barraged with options as to how to quench our thirst. We are buried in advertisements and information and suggestions and ideas and products and programs and have you heard the latest? Catalogs and flyers are felling forests to offer an answer to our ache, to assuage our thirst.

I have tried a lot of them. I've bought the shoes, read the book, done the study, and attended the program. I'm still thirsty. Scientists warn that the ability to be aware of and respond to thirst is slowly blunted as we age. In a world that oftentimes feels as dry as a desert, we can become numb to our own thirst.

But as women who are being transformed into the image of Christ, we don't want to grow numb but increasingly thirsty. I've tried to assuage my thirsty heart. I still need something to drink. I need the Living Water himself. So do you. This is our most precious fundamental need. Jesus invites, "Let anyone who is thirsty come to me and drink" (John 7:37 NIV 2011).

learning from Mary

The fount my mother drank from flowed for her in the Catholic Church. Particularly she had an affinity for Mary, the mother of Jesus. And really, in any Nativity play, what little girl does not want to play Mary? Clearly, she is the star of that show. Okay, Jesus is the Star, but in elementary school a doll plays his part. Mary's is the coveted role. My mother had statues of Mary in her bedroom. She encouraged me to pray to Mary and ask her to intervene on my behalf with her son. "Jesus will listen to Mary. Every good son listens to his mother."

There's always been a good bit of tension between Catholics and Protestants when it comes to Mary. Mom and I had many conversations where I encouraged her to just go ahead and talk with Jesus directly. He invites us to do that. But no, she felt Mary would understand her needs better and more convincingly convey them to her son. I rebelled a little. I wouldn't pray to Mary, and I still don't. But I also didn't recognize the fount of wisdom that Mary is. Not until I was a grown woman myself did I take a deeper look at the life of Mary and become inspired, awed, and encouraged. Now she is one of my favorite women ever. I look forward to meeting her.

Mary was a woman of unshakable faith, immense wisdom, and profound courage. But she was also not that different from us. She was thirsty too. And she risked everything for a drink. The more I know about Mary, the more I want to be like her.

We can imagine that her parents misunderstood her as a teenager. When she turned up pregnant but still claimed to be a virgin, most likely they didn't believe she was telling the truth. And if they didn't, who could blame them? "Hi, Mom; hi, Dad. I'm pregnant. No, I haven't ever known a man. The child I carry is the Son of God sent to save the world." Sure, Mary. No problem.

It is safe to say we can relate to Mary in that there were times when she had trouble with her parents. She had trouble with her fiancé. They came close to divorce. We can guess that she was misunderstood and judged by her community. Did anyone other than Joseph believe her story? Mary became a widow as so many women do while she herself had many years left ahead of her. She had her share of troubles in raising her children. She can relate to us.

We are familiar with her debut. Mary was a young woman between thirteen and fifteen years old when the angel Gabriel appeared to her and said, "Greetings, you who are highly favored! The Lord is with you" (Luke 1:28). Luke merely says, "Mary was greatly troubled at his words" (v. 29). Wouldn't you be?

Granted, the scene is hard to imagine. Christian producers and pagan filmmakers alike have tried to capture this moment, but Hollywood has not been able to do it. How could they? Heaven broke into Mary's life unexpectedly and without the fanfare of trumpets. The angel was sent to her. Where? Did Gabriel suddenly appear in her bedroom? Did he walk up to her at a stream? We don't know. We do know that Mary knew he was an angel and that she was amazingly calm.

The angel continued to give her startling news:

> Do not be afraid, Mary, you have found favor with God.
> You will be with child and give birth to a son, and you are
> to give him the name Jesus. He will be great and will be
> called the Son of the Most High. The Lord God will give
> him the throne of his father David, and he will reign over
> the house of Jacob forever; his kingdom will never end.
> (vv. 30–33)

No matter how troubled Mary was, her heart had been cultivated by faith, and she responded to the news with composure, dignity, and faith. She did not scream or fall on her face. She simply asked the angel a question: "How will this be ... since I am a virgin?" (v. 34).

She asked with expectancy. "How *will* God do this, with me being a virgin and all?" It is not a question of doubt. It is a question *rooted in faith*. Mary immediately believed Gabriel. She did not laugh as Sarah did when she overheard the conversation between her husband and the Lord that she in her old age would bear a son. When confronted with the miraculous, Mary asked how *will*.

Unbeknownst to Mary, this same angel had visited her relative Zechariah and brought him astonishing, impossible news. When Gabriel told Zechariah that he and Elizabeth in their old age would have a son, an amazing son, Zechariah asked, "How can this be?" (v. 18, author's paraphrase). Not how will; how *can*. The difference exposed his heart. He did not believe the angel, and it did not go well for him. Mary was blessed by the angel above all women. Zechariah was struck dumb.

Mary asked, "How will?" She knew that if God says something—anything—we can believe him. God is true. He is trustworthy. Jesus is a man of his Word.

Mary knew God before she ever carried him in her womb. Before the angel ever spoke those words, she knew that nothing is impossible for God.

Her response: "Behold the maidservant of the Lord! Let it happen to me according to your word" (v. 38 MOUNCE).

In other words, *I belong to him. I am his. So yes, Lord.* Her spirit was a big ole yes to God. Did she know what this was going to mean for her? Maybe. Was she afraid? Maybe. She was a human being. Just like us, she was not perfect. She knew better than anyone else her weaknesses. And God chose her. He chose her to bring the Savior of the world to the world just as God has chosen us to bring the Savior of the world to our world. Mary said, "You know best!" She trusted God and believed that he is good. She believed God and knew that he was worthy of her yes.

Mary was a very young woman of very profound faith. How good it is to follow in her footsteps. To respond as she did and believe. In *My Utmost for His Highest*, Oswald Chambers wrote,

> We are not uncertain of God, but uncertain of what He will do next. If we are only certain in our beliefs we get dignified and severe and have the ban of finality about our views but when we are rightly related to God, life is full of spontaneous, joyful uncertainty and expectancy.[3]

Our life of faith is uncertain, but we can be expectant of good. Because we belong to God, we can rest in knowing his promises to us are true and he is faithful. It's not a question of if God is going to show up but how and when. It is not a question of *if* he is going to move on our behalf but *how* he will. It isn't even a question of if he is going to continue pursuing and wooing us deeper into his heart filled with affection for us but if we will recognize him. We can live with joyful uncertainty and expectancy. There are no ifs with God. The only ifs relate to us.

If we trust him.

If we believe him.

If we ask him.

If we continue to ask him.

How God loves his people to ask him in faith—pressing in, continuing to ask no matter how long it takes, believing that he will come through for us. I just got off the phone with a friend who has been praying for her children to come to know Jesus for thirty years. Sometimes she loses hope and needs others to carry her hope for a while. But she continues to pray and believe. She's right to do so. Because, really, what's too difficult for God? A virgin giving birth? God himself becoming a man and living among us? Flooding the whole earth, maybe? Or coming for you? Coming to you in your thirst and in your uncertainty? The angel Gabriel said, "For with God nothing will be impossible" (Luke 1:37 WBT).

The miraculous is not a strange thing to God. *The miraculous is his normal.* Divinely interrupting our lives is not an extraordinary event. Supernaturally showing up, speaking into the heart, and creating a longing for himself—this is his realm. He speaks to us. He leads us. He heals us. He presses into us with his manifest presence as we reach out to him. He moves through us with power, revealing his glory. God has come. God will come. God loves to come.

God likes rescuing his people. He enjoys coming through in dramatic ways. The stories we find in Scripture are rife with him stacking the deck against his ability to rescue or save and then ... POW! He proves himself amazing and involved once again.

I am asking him now to come for our hearts, to come for our thirst, and I am not going to ask how can he come but expect that he will.

what Mary pondered

One of the next times we meet Mary is on the night of Jesus's birth. The shepherds have come to seek her son. They tell her and Joseph of the angel's proclamation. How encouraging that must have been! Thank God for his confirmations. Afterward, Scripture says, "Mary treasured up all these things and pondered them in her heart" (Luke 2:19 NKJV).

I love that Mary treasured them in her heart. She was familiar with the prophecies. Mary *actively remembered.* Late at night, while nursing her little baby, she would pull out these treasures and think on them. She was a woman of wisdom who knew what to store in her heart, what to treasure, what to ponder.

So it's a good thing to ask ourselves, what are we pondering? When it's late at night and we can't sleep. When all is quiet outside of you, what is going on inside of you? In the stillness of your own soul, if you can even get it to be still—not going through the to-do lists for the next day—what is treasured there for you to pull up and ponder? For many of us it's our failures, our disappointments of the day, the week, the month, our lives. Or often it's not our own failures but the failures of others who have disappointed us.

Those are not treasures. Their names are accusations, regrets, resentments. Pondering on these will not bring life to our thirsty souls. I know I'm not the only woman who late at night has thought of the perfect thing to say, days after the conversation. Or who has had a brilliant conversation with someone who isn't there. I have learned something: it is not a good idea to have conversations with people who are not actually in the room. As I mentioned in chapter 8, when we do that, our spirit reaches out to them and builds a bridge to them, and all of their warfare, or anger, or sorrows come traveling across that bridge back to us. Those are ungodly soul ties.

Should you find yourself doing it again, remember to catch yourself, release the people to God, bless them in Jesus's Name, and let them go. Entrust them to Jesus, and then command your spirit to come home to the Spirit of God in your body. Then tell God your sorrows. Have your conversation with him! He actually is in the room with you.

Treasures are true. They are what Paul encourages us to ponder: "Whatever is noble, whatever is right, whatever is pure, whatever is lovely, whatever is admirable—if anything is excellent or praiseworthy—think about such things" (Phil. 4:8). Think on these things! Treasures are Scripture. Treasures include remembering what God has said and done and promised he will do. The greatest treasure of all is Jesus himself. What about lying in bed and thinking about him?

Try it tonight. Let your imagination—consecrated to Jesus—go. How handsome he is! How strong! How brave! How courageous, bold, noble, kingly, and glorious! What a great singer he is! What a great dancer! You name it, he's the best at it! And he wants you! You—yes, you—have been chosen by the King of Kings. Ponder that.

Mary was a woman of great wisdom. She knew what to treasure. She knew what to ponder.

what Mary suffered

Let's go back to when Joseph and Mary brought Jesus to the temple to be dedicated. You may remember: Simeon and Anna both prophesied powerfully over Jesus. When Simeon was finished he looked at Mary and said, "And a sword will pierce your own soul" (Luke 2:35).

Cheery.

There are several possible interpretations of what he meant. Was he telling her how she would die? We don't know. But we do know that her soul was pierced as only a mother's heart can be pierced at the torture and death of her firstborn son.

Jesus told us that in this life we will all have suffering. He is not speaking merely of the huge things that happen, but also of the innumerable, persistent, smaller sorrows that press one upon the other and shape our souls. Perhaps Simeon had these in mind as well.

We women were given a huge capacity and need for relationship. It is our glory and a beautiful way that we bear the image of God, who enjoys perfect, intimate relationship. But our glory has been tainted. Because of human brokenness and sin, there is not one relationship in your life that is not touched at some level by disappointment. There is an undercurrent of sorrow in every woman's life.

Oftentimes, when I feel this sorrow, this loneliness, I think it is revealing something deeply wrong with me. I think that if I was "doing it right" or if *I* was all right, then I wouldn't experience this grief. And yes, like you, I am not all that I am meant to be yet. I am becoming. But when I ache, if I believe the cause rests solely on my failures, it is overwhelming. I must run from it. Hide it. Manage it. Sanctify it. Ignore it. Numb it. Or better yet, kill it! Because when I am awake to it, it hurts. And I can feel bad for feeling bad. Sound familiar?

The undercurrent of sorrow that we feel is not all our fault. Maybe a part of it is. Maybe God is using it to expose a style of relating that he wants us to repent of. Maybe. But it's also possible that none of the sorrow we are feeling at a given moment is rooted in our failings. When we become aware of sadness or disappointment, we do not have to run. Sorrow is one of the realities of life. To be mature women, we have to be awake to the ache. Let it be a doorway for us to walk through to find deeper intimacy with God. We ask God to meet us—right in the ache.

When we are the most awake to our hearts, we are closest to the glory intended for us. We are not demanding. We are not running. We acquire a depth to our souls and become free to really love others. We become women of mercy, knowing that those around us ache as well.

I used to think I was the only person who underneath it all was profoundly lonely. Then I learned it is a relational ache shared by all women. And then I learned it is shared by every human being. Jesus is well acquainted with loneliness. He knows the sorrow of being judged unfairly.

He knows well what grief it is being left all alone and not wanting to be alone. Remember the garden of Gethsemane? John Milton said, "Loneliness is the first thing which God's eye named, not good."[4]

"The whole conviction of my life," wrote Thomas Wolfe, "now rests upon the belief that loneliness, far from being a rare and curious phenomenon, peculiar to myself and to a few other solitary men, is the central and inevitable fact of human existence."[5]

God put this ache in us. He wants us to be awake to it and let it achieve its purpose of drawing our hearts to Jesus. Let us allow sorrow to become a tool in the hand of our God to lead us to the Man of Sorrows himself.

One day during recess when I was six years old, the ring finger on my right hand got caught in a slamming door. There was this mysterious storage shed out on the playground, and I was sneakily investigating. I risked opening the door but then got scared and let go. It snapped shut and almost cut off my finger.

The only thing revealing the injury to my finger was a single drop of blood. But it hurt. I went to my teacher, and she took me to the bathroom to clean it off. When she put my finger under the running water, the skin peeled back, exposing the bone, and we both were stunned. My mother was called. I don't remember my mother picking me up, but I do remember lying on the examining table with my mom standing by my side. I was kicking myself with one leg, tears streaming down my face in agony as the doctor shot something directly into my wound. It was excruciating. My mom had tears streaming down her cheeks too. And she was saying, "It's hurting me more than it's hurting you."

As a child I didn't understand how that was possible. But forty-five years later, as a mother myself, I do. It is one thing to endure pain yourself. It is quite another to watch someone you love endure pain and be utterly helpless to change it. You know what I'm talking about. Whether it is your child or your parent, your husband or your precious friend, it can hurt us more than it's hurting them.

Blaine and Sam were sick at the same time, as children usually are. Luke wasn't born yet. Sam was almost four, Blaine not yet two, when we packed them into the car to take them to the doctor. As we were driving down Garden of the Gods Road, a strange sound came from the back seat. I turned around to see Blaine having a seizure. His first. It terrified me. I didn't know what it was. I thought he was dying. I started calling his name and pleading with him to stay with me. John pulled over to the side of the road only to have me scream at him, "Go! Go!"

When a desperate father runs into the emergency room, carrying a limp, unconscious child, you don't have to sign in. We were barely in the door when a nurse rushed to us and led us to an examining room. Chaos ensued. Doctors hustled about in skilled lifesaving mode. Nurses moved precisely and quickly. John and I were terrified. And then Blaine came to.

I tell this story mindful that you may have endured much, much worse.

The doctors wanted to test Blaine for meningitis. I wasn't sure. We spoke with several doctors, we prayed, and then we took all their advice and agreed. Blaine was strapped facedown to a board, and we were told to leave the room. We dutifully obeyed,

I regret that.

In a test for meningitis, a long needle is inserted into the spine for fluid to be drawn out, and it is extremely painful. In his pain and terror, Blaine called out, "Mom! Mom!" They told him, "Your mother isn't here." So Blaine began to yell, "Dad! Dad!" We didn't come.

Knowing that hurts me more than it hurt him.

Where was Mary when Jesus was crucified? You know where she was. She was right there with him. She was faithful to her son but helpless, unable to intervene in any way. Mary's heart was pierced all right. She must have been in excruciating pain while she stood at the foot of her son's cross. Mary remained with her gaze locked on her son, the son she had carried and nursed and raised and loved. The son she knew was the Holy One of Israel. The Messiah. The Son of God. The son who now was dying in agony. Mary was there. Did she think it was hurting her more than it was hurting him? Was it?

Three of the gospel accounts say that while Jesus was being crucified, there were women there who stood at a distance: "the women who followed him from Galilee, stood at a distance, watching these things" (Luke 23:49). But John's gospel says his mother did not stand at a distance: "Near the cross of Jesus stood his mother, his mother's sister, Mary the wife of Clopas, and Mary Magdalene" (John 19:25).

Jesus did not have to look far into the distance to see his mother. He just had to glance down. One of Jesus's last sentences concerned Mary. He spoke to the beloved apostle John: "Behold your mother" (v. 27 NKJV). He loved Mary in his agony. He looked to her future in his agony as he looks to ours.

My first ten years as a mother included our share of injuries, stitches, broken bones, emergency-room visits in the middle of the night, ambulance rides, hospital stays, and two heart surgeries. And my children are mostly healthy. But a sword has pierced my heart. I know that a sword has pierced yours, too. A sword pierced Mary's heart, but she was able to carry on. We shall be able to, as well, because Jesus's eye is also on us.

what Mary obeyed

When Jesus began his ministry, it was at a wedding feast. You may know the story. It was a neighbor's or a friend's—anyway, it was a big event. His mother was there.

There was a problem: they ran out of wine. Mary knew who could fix that! No more wine? No problem! She told Jesus, "They have no more wine" (John 2:3). His response was, "Dear woman, why do you involve me? … My time has not yet come" (v. 4).

It makes me wonder about his home life, those thirty years veiled by silence. I imagine Mary getting ready to make bread, no one but Jesus at home, and they have run out of money and out of oil. *Jesus! Come here! We're out of oil.* It might have happened. We do know that all she had to do was say to Jesus, "They're out of wine." He said, "So?" Then she turned to the servants and said, "Do whatever he tells you" (v. 5).

Now that is very good advice. Can you hear her? She is telling us the same thing: "Do whatever he tells you." He is good. He is powerful. He is love. He knows what he is doing. We can trust him.

We hear of Mary again when she and her sons go to talk with Jesus:

> Then Jesus' mother and brothers arrived. Standing out-
> side, they sent someone in to call him. A crowd was sitting
> around him, and they told him, "Your mother and broth-
> ers are outside looking for you." (Mark 3:31–32)

His mother wanted to have a word with him. Some gospels say his family thought he had lost his mind. His mother and brothers didn't understand the intensity with which he was ministering. Perhaps they were concerned that he was not taking care of himself. Mark reported that "so many people were coming and going that they did not even have a chance to eat" (6:31). Remember that Mary was a human being. She was not perfect, and she was first and foremost his *mother*; a Jewish mother worried that her son was not getting enough to eat. Mary had her moments, just like we have our moments, when she doubted her son. She was not sure that *what* he was doing and *the way* he was doing it were really the best.

Haven't we all been unsure ourselves? I know I have gone knocking on heaven's door—"Can I have a word with you? I think you're missing something important here." Jesus is unfazed by our doubt, and he was unfazed by his mother's. But we know that Mary did not remain in doubt.

She knew who Jesus was. She stayed with him, followed him, and stood by him until the very end.

The last time we hear of Mary in the Scriptures is in Acts. In all probability, she had seen Jesus resurrected, and she was gathered with the disciples, devoted to prayer, and present when the Holy Spirit was poured out at Pentecost! After that, we don't hear about Mary anymore. But we can imagine. We can ponder. We can imitate.

She was a woman of faith, a woman of immense courage, obedience, and wisdom. She was a woman well acquainted with sorrow, who knew who Jesus was, followed hard after him *no matter what*, and encouraged others to do the same. We can imagine her speaking to us now:

Do whatever he tells you to do! And when he tells you, don't ask "how can?" but always "how will?"

12

becoming a woman
of worship

Our dog, Oban, loves me best.

He's a five-year-old golden retriever, and I'm his favorite. He pouts when I'm not home and stays in his cozy crate, uninterested in the happenings of the day—though not all that much is happening during the quiet of the weekday hours. But still he pouts. When I am home, Oban follows me around and lies down at my feet wherever I happen to be sitting: in the living-room chair, at my desk, or at the kitchen table. He's at my feet even now. Oban follows me around because he adores me. And although I'd like to believe my dog's affection has absolutely nothing to do with the fact that I am the only one who feeds him, I know it has everything to do with it. Oban's attentiveness is simply him loving me in response to the way I have loved him and hoping that I may at any moment love him again by way of a biscuit.

Oban is a very smart dog. He knows where it will benefit him the most to focus his attention. We are, all of us, way smarter than my dog. Jesus has captured our attention, and now we are women who want to sit at *his* feet. To help prepare our hearts to receive what Jesus wants to say to us in this chapter, let's begin by praying.

> *Dear Jesus,*
>> *I come under your authority.*
>> *I come under your love.*
>> *I give myself to you utterly.*
>> *I lay down everything that I've been carrying and give myself to you:*
>> *my heart, mind, soul, body, and spirit—everything in me.*
>> *Please cleanse me afresh with your blood.*
>> *I ask your Spirit to restore my union with you!*
>> *Fill me with your Life! Give me eyes to see and ears to hear you.*
>> *Remove everything that is in between you and me, Jesus.*
>> *I love you.*
>> *It's in your mighty Name that I pray.*
>> *Amen.*

what Jesus longs for

What is it that Jesus wants? What does he want more than anything else? Well, that's an easy one because he hasn't exactly kept it a secret. Jesus wants us to love him. Remember when Jesus was asked, "Which is the greatest commandment?" (Matt. 22:36). He answered, "Love the Lord your God with all your heart and with all your soul and with all your mind" (v. 37). Love God! Jesus is God. He is saying, "Love me! The most important and highest thing you can do with all of your life is to love me!"

Here's a fascinating thing: you reflect the heart of God. You are made in his image, right? Down to your feminine core, you express something about the heart of God to the world. And what does every woman's heart long for? To be loved. To be chosen. To be a priority to someone. Think of how deeply this runs in you. Now you know something really central about the heart of God. He wants that too.

Voluntarily offering our love to God is the most important thing we can do. Loving Jesus is the fire that fuels every other good work in our lives. And loving God enables us to live a courageous life that can't help but spill out onto others. Let's look into the Scriptures and learn from a woman who loved God first and with everything she had: Mary of Bethany.

Mary of Bethany was Lazarus's sister. The other half of Mary and Martha. She knew Jesus well. And because she knew him well, she loved him much. (Loving Jesus is simply the heart's natural response to knowing him.)

My mother hated the famous story of Mary and Martha. She thought Martha was unappreciated, and who of us doesn't agree at some level? *Somebody* had to cook the meal! Women usually find themselves in the kitchen at gatherings either preparing the food or cleaning it up. I know I do. I'm often more comfortable there. So yes, I relate to Martha too. A little more deeply than I care to admit.

But in this story Martha represents a busy and distracted church. She is a picture of us when we have exchanged relationship with Jesus for service of him.

> As Jesus and his disciples were on their way, he came to a village where a woman named Martha opened her home to him. She had a sister called Mary, who sat at the Lord's feet listening to what he said. But Martha was distracted by all the preparations that had to be made. She came to him and asked, "Lord, don't you care that my sister has left me to do the work by myself? Tell her to help me!"

"Martha, Martha," the Lord answered, "you are worried and upset about many things, but only one thing is
needed. Mary has chosen what is better, and it will not be
taken away from her." (Luke 10:38–42)

Martha criticized her sister and rebuked the Lord. "Why are you just
sitting there? Do you not see what is going on here? I am working *so* hard,
and my sister is doing *nothing*. Make her help me." I love how Jesus gently
corrected Martha for her worry and distraction. He didn't say that what
Martha was doing was wrong, but that her attitude was. (Probably a good
clue that we may be off in our attitudes is when we feel compelled to rebuke
God for not intervening!)

But Mary's focus was undivided. She wasn't being lazy. She'd been captured. She wasn't running about helping her sister because she was smitten
with Jesus. She had chosen to learn from Jesus, to listen to his words, to
open her heart and her mind to him. She was doing the one thing that was
required—loving Jesus. And Jesus applauded her choice.

My family says I have ruined Oban because of my habit of giving him
samples of what I'm eating. He loves to share an apple with me. A bite for
me, a chunk for him. Oban isn't a very picky eater. He will eat anything.
And by anything, I do mean *anything*. Dirty socks are a favorite. But above
all Oban wants what *you* are eating. So now, when anyone is eating, particularly if it is an apple, Oban will sit at their feet as well, eyes glued to
their food, utterly and completely focused. He is captured. And maybe it's
not the most flattering picture, but he reminds me of Mary. Nothing is
going to distract that dog from the most important thing that is going on
around him! He will sit with the undivided focus of a passionate disciple.

Mary sat at Jesus's feet, which is the sign of a disciple. (I love how Jesus
is with women! It was scandalous at that time and remains scandalous in
so many places today to have a woman disciple. But Jesus had them. He

esteems women.) Rather than being busy doing things for him, Mary was simply being *with* him. And Jesus said that being with him, listening to him, honoring him with her attention and adoration, was far above doing things for him. "Martha, Martha ... Mary has chosen what is better, and it will not be taken from her."

Jesus *defended* Mary's choice. He didn't get angry with Martha either, by the way. He simply invited her to the better choice by presenting it to her.

Jesus doesn't pant after our service, as wonderful as it is. As much as he has planted desires and dreams in our hearts, he doesn't give first place to the use of our gifts to further the kingdom of God or to minister to his beloved lambs. Jesus says that the greatest command is to love him. We love him by loving others, yes, but God gives first place to our loving him, and we do that simply by *being* with him, spending time with him, fixing our gaze on who he is.

You know that when you really love someone, it gives you great joy just to be in the same room with them. Our sons no longer live at home, and when they do come home for a visit, I am so happy! Just to have them under the same roof as me makes me glad. My heart rests in the joy of their proximity. You know this. Mary knew this. Jesus knows this too.

I love you, I trust you

One of the next times we encounter Mary of Bethany in the Scriptures is after the death of her cherished brother, Lazarus. Jesus loved Lazarus. He loved Mary and Martha, too, but he didn't rush to Lazarus's side when he heard that he was sick. Jesus chose to wait two more days before traveling to Bethany. The sisters wanted him to come and heal Lazarus. But Jesus had something even better in mind.

So he waited. And then he performed one of the greatest miracles of his earthly ministry. Just like we have had to do so many times, Mary and

Martha had to wait for God to come. Waiting for God is one of the hardest things we ever have to do, isn't it? But if Jesus had come right away and healed Lazarus, we all would have missed out.

Believing God is good in the midst of waiting is incredibly hard. Believing God is good in the midst of immense sorrow, loss, or pain is even more difficult. Those are the times that our faith, the treasure of our hearts, is tested by fire and becomes gold. What we come to know of God and the terrain he comes to inhabit in our hearts through the trial leads people to say, "I wouldn't change a thing." That's the crazy, supernatural realm of God.

I know that there have been many times when God didn't answer your prayers in the way you wanted or in the timing you wanted. But what he did in the end was far better. Even if the "far better" was your coming to depend on him more deeply through the travail.

All of us are living lives that are wondrous and filled with heartaches. That is real. I can only imagine what you are living in … waiting for … longing for … weeping for. Holding on to your faith for. I know what I am living in. Gold is being forged, gals. Priceless, immeasurable gold. To paraphrase Philip Yancey: faith believes ahead of time what can only be seen by looking back.[1] There will come a day when we will look back and understand. But in the waiting, may God strengthen our hearts to hold on to his.

Lazarus had been dead for four days when Jesus finally came to town. And I love that when Martha heard he had come, she ran out to meet him. Martha may get a raw deal sometimes, but she was running to him in this moment. She loved Jesus. She said, "Lord … if you had been here, my brother would not have died" (John 11:21). And then she said,

> "But I know that even now God will give you whatever you ask."…
> Jesus said to her, "I am the resurrection and the life. He who believes in me will live, even though he dies; and

whoever lives and believes in me will never die. Do you believe this?"

"Yes, Lord," she told him, "I believe that you are the Christ, the Son of God, who was to come into the world." (vv. 22–27)

Theologians call this the threefold confession. It was the highest confession that Martha could make. Yay, Martha! And don't you love how she said, "But I know that *even now* God will give you whatever you ask"? Martha was still holding out her hope for the miraculous intervention of Jesus.

Mary didn't come. She stayed in the house, grieving. She didn't go to Jesus until she was told that he was asking after her. Mary was a real person. She wasn't this amazing I-do-it-all-right-all-the-time gal. She was a woman like you and me who, when overcome by grief, sometimes cannot even move. Mary couldn't move, not until she was called out by her God.

Mary loved Jesus. She ran to him then and fell at his feet. She worshipped him. She brought to Jesus the whole truth of who she was, including her profound grief and uncontrolled weeping. And in seeing her weeping, the Scripture says, Jesus was "deeply moved" (v. 33). Jesus was moved by the heartfelt tears of one who loved him, and he is moved by yours as well.

Did you hear me? Jesus is moved by your tears, your love, your waiting, and your sorrows. He is moved when you trust him even though it all looks hopeless. It is one of the deepest ways we express our love for him.

Martha and Mary laid out their hearts before Jesus. And they chose to trust him. You know what happened next!

lavish loving

Days later, when Jesus was again having dinner with the very much alive Lazarus, and Martha was ... well, serving, Mary did the unthinkable.

She came quietly into the room with an alabaster jar of very expensive perfume. (And by the way, she wasn't at home. She was at Simon the Leper's house. Mary brought the oil with her. She planned this ahead of time!) Many commentators believe this perfume was her life savings. Mary broke the neck of the jar open and slowly poured some of the perfume on Jesus's head and then poured the rest on his feet. Then she did something extremely intimate and scandalous. She unbound her hair and wiped his feet with it, even though a respectable woman did not let down her hair in public.

Mary was not concerned with what anyone else thought. She had an undivided heart. She poured out all she had onto Jesus in an extravagant offering of worship. She spent herself on him. She ministered to him in a culturally significant way. Nowadays, pouring all of your Chanel No. 5 onto someone you think highly of might well end that relationship, but what Mary did was a recognizable offering of worship.

There were several immediate results.

First, the fragrance of her offering filled the room. There was a *change in the atmosphere*. When we pour out all we have in worship to Jesus, the beauty of that offering can be sensed by those around us. It is an alluring fragrance that lingers.

Early in Acts, the Pharisees were amazed at the courage of Peter and John. Peter and John spoke with power, and the Pharisees noted that these men had been with Jesus. When we worship Jesus, when we are with him, the fragrance of his love fills our hearts and spills over. The atmosphere changes within us and around us. Just as the Pharisees could tell, people can tell that we have been with Jesus.

The second thing that happened after Mary ministered to Jesus was that the disciples rebuked her. Over and over again, Jesus had told his disciples that he would be killed in Jerusalem and then rise. But they didn't understand. The opposition to Jesus was growing stronger every day. There was a contract out on his life. He was being hunted. It was attentive Mary who sat at the Lord's feet who knew there was not much time left. There was nothing Mary owned that she would not spend on him.

The Gospels tell us that those present were indignant and rebuked her harshly. *What a waste of money! A whole year's wages poured out for nothing! Think of how many poor families could eat for a week on that.* They saw only money. Mary saw only Jesus.

Have you ever had your motives misunderstood? Have you ever had someone criticize the way you worship or spend your time or money, the way you minister or believe or come through or don't come through? It has happened to me countless times, and I hate it. Jesus isn't so fond of it either. When people judge you, that is. Especially for loving him. Jesus knows well that it hurts to be misunderstood and judged. He knows that it is part of the sorrow of living in a fallen world.

We hurt others when we interpret their actions through lenses of mis-understanding wrought in our brokenness and sin. We are hurt by others when they do it to us. And when it happens to us, how are we supposed to defend ourselves? What did Mary do? Well, Mary didn't say a word in her own defense—but Jesus did. Jesus always defends a worshipper. Sometimes God will ask us to speak—in love—but always he is our Defender.

> "Leave her alone," said Jesus. "Why are you bothering her? She has done a beautiful thing to me. The poor you will always have with you, and you can help them any time you want. But you will not always have me. She did what she could. She poured perfume on my body beforehand to prepare for my burial. I tell you the truth, wherever the gospel is preached throughout the world, what she has done will also be told, in memory of her." (Mark 14:6–9)

Jesus defended Mary's reckless devotion. Jesus "got" Mary, and he "gets" you. He understood her heart and the depth of her love. He said, "She has done a beautiful thing *to* me." He never said that about anyone or anything else. What was the beautiful thing? She spent all her love on him.

But did you notice what else Jesus said? "She did what she could." She had her unique portion, and she gave it all. There is grace here for us to receive, gals. We are not the same. Comparing ourselves to one another leads to death. We are each given a portion. We are given our part to play. We are a body. We need each other. *We do what we can.*

The Gospels don't mention this Mary again. She wasn't at the crucifixion or the empty tomb. This Mary who was inside her home grieving the loss of her brother Lazarus after his death and unable to run to meet Jesus is the same woman who knew that Jesus was going to die—and believed he was going to be raised on the third day. But her heart could not take seeing it happen.

By the way, Mary's love offering would have lingered. The fragrance of the oil Mary had poured out on Jesus days before was still on his hair, his feet, and wherever else it dripped. Mary wasn't at the crucifixion, but the beauty of her offering was.

Mary understood the times, she had amazing faith, and she ministered to Jesus in a way that no one else even comprehended, because she knew him. She loved him. She worshipped him lavishly.

And Jesus *loved* it.

scandalous love

Finally, let's see what we can glean from the life of one more of my favorite women, Mary Magdalene.

Church tradition identifies her as the one who trespassed into the Pharisee's dinner party and kissed Jesus's feet while she washed them with her tears and dried them with her hair. The Pharisee and his guests were aghast, but Jesus defended her. (Remember, Jesus always defends his worshipper.) But actually, there's no scriptural basis to believe this was Mary Magdalene. This scandalous lover of God was a different fabulous woman.

Mary Magdalene, we do know, was a woman whom Jesus delivered of seven demons. What woman would not be grateful? She was also a woman of some means who had followed Jesus from Galilee. It was unthinkable to have women travel with men in those times—especially single women with single men! But Jesus was completely unconcerned with the traditions of society, and he is still unconcerned with them. Mary and several other women traveled with him and his disciples, "helping to support them out of their own means" (Luke 8:3).

Mary Magdalene was passionate in her devotion to Jesus. Yes, she traveled with him. Mary needed to be with Jesus because she loved him. And she, along with Jesus's mother, the disciple John, and a few other women followed Jesus as he made his way to Golgotha. Mary Magdalene stayed with him at the cross. Peter didn't. The Sons of Thunder didn't. John did, and so did Jesus's mother and a handful of women.

You have probably seen photos of Michelangelo's beautiful carving *The Pietà*, which portrays Jesus's mother holding the broken body of Jesus after his crucifixion. It is beautiful and heart wrenching, but it isn't true. Women didn't remove Jesus's body from the cross or even handle him. Men did. Joseph of Arimathea and Nicodemus got permission to take Jesus's body, and they laid him in the tomb.

Mary Magdalene didn't know these men. Nicodemus and Joseph were disciples of Jesus in secret. She was also not familiar with this tomb. So she sneaked after them, following at a distance so she would know exactly where they put Jesus's body. She couldn't bear not knowing. The separation from Jesus was excruciating. So on the third day, at the crack of dawn, at the first possible moment, Mary and a few other women went back to the tomb with spices and oil to minister to Jesus's body. To their utter dismay, they discovered that the tomb was empty.

Mary was frantic: "They have taken the Lord out of the tomb, and we don't know where they have put him!" (John 20:2).

She saw a man, assumed he was the gardener, and asked him if he had taken the body. And then Jesus revealed himself to her simply by saying her name, "Mary" (v. 16). Her response? She fell at his feet and worshipped him. Mary forever has the honor of being the first person to worship the risen and victorious Lord.

Mary Magdalene was a worshipper. She had been healed and delivered of much, and she loved Jesus thoroughly. She followed him. She gave her complete focus. She gave her resources. She gave her heart. She gave her unconditional surrender.

This is what Jesus most longs for. He's not panting after your sacrifice or even your obedience. He doesn't need your money. He doesn't need your gifting. Oh, but he wants your heart. He longs for your love. Our adoration is the *one thing* we possess that he cannot claim without our offering it to him. Jesus longs for you to come close to him. And he has been moving throughout all eternity, battling, suffering, dying, and triumphing to win your heart for himself. He wants to capture your heart as a response to his overwhelming love for *you*.

Mary Magdalene knew this. Jesus wants us to know it too.

It wasn't merely a coincidence that Jesus revealed himself first to Mary Magdalene. She didn't just bump into him as he was walking out of the tomb. He wasn't simply still in the neighborhood. The risen Savior is no longer bound by the constraints of time and space. The resurrected Jesus walks through walls. He appears and disappears suddenly. Jesus *chose* to appear to Mary first. He chose her. Why?

Is his heart not drawn to the hearts of those who love him?

Have you ever been chosen? Over lots of other people? Picked first for the dodgeball team? Asked to a dance? Selected for the cheer squad? Given a choice role in the school play, a promotion, an award? It is a wonderful thing to be chosen. Growing up, I wasn't athletic. I was never picked first for the team, and I was never once asked to a dance.

However, when I was in the fourth grade I was chosen by my classmates to be Citizen of the Year. I still remember the joy of it. Each day the teacher chose one student to be Citizen of the Day. Their name went up on the special chart for all to see. On the last day of school the teacher tallied up the names to see who had won the honor most often. It turned out to be a tie between me and a cute boy named Bobby. So she took a private vote. The thing was, there were more boys in the classroom than girls, so I was pretty certain I wouldn't win.

But I had an edge. My family was moving in a week or so from our home in Prairie Village, Kansas, to unknown California. I was leaving, and everyone knew it. This could be my good-bye present. And I did win.

At the time I thought it was a sympathy vote, or it could have been that I was just more citizen-ly than he was, but I didn't really care why I won. I simply cared that *I* was chosen. My prize was a certificate and the cardboard sheet with the school photos of all my classmates. I took their photos off the board, put them in an envelope, and brought them with me to California.

I was chosen immediately before a separation from my friends and caregivers in what would become the earthquake of my young life. When we got to our new state, my family utterly fell apart. How many times did I go to my little box and pour over my classmates' pictures and remember that I was loved and that there was a place where people knew and cared for me? I had been chosen. It was a God-given lifeline of remembrance when I needed it most.

You have been chosen too.

You did not choose me, but I chose you. (John 15:16)

For he chose us in him before the creation of the world.
(Eph. 1:4)

God's chosen people, holy and dearly loved. (Col. 3:12)

It is important for us to let our hearts rest in that.

Jesus stayed with his disciples for forty wondrous days after his resurrection. But then, as we know all too well, he left. He ascended into heaven and gave his followers instructions to stay together and wait.

Mary Magdalene was with them. Gathered with them. Praying. Waiting. Not knowing what she was waiting for, exactly, but knowing that Jesus had spoken about the Holy Spirit. Imagine those ten days. Jesus was gone. The Holy Spirit was not living inside them. They could not hear Jesus's still small voice. They could not sense his presence. They were empty. But Jesus had given them a promise. He told them that the promised Holy Spirit was coming, and they believed him. And so they waited. And in the waiting, they held on to the truth. They remembered, and they reminded each other. Each one of them had been chosen and set apart.

God has given us all kinds of promises. Some have come true and we are living in them, and some we are waiting for. And in the waiting, in the longing, in the aching, in the living and the loving, we must *remember*. We remember Jesus, and we cling to him. We remember the promises he has given us. And the hope to which he has called us. And we remind one another.

love as worship

One of the best ways to help us remember who our God is and who we are to him is to worship him. In worship, when we turn the gaze of our hearts away from ourselves and our needs and onto Jesus, a divine shift happens that brings a great good to our lives. Our enormous struggles and concerns become much less overwhelming in the face of our powerful, loving Jesus. In worship, we remember that we have been bought with his precious blood. We remember who we belong to.

You are Jesus's beloved: "I belong to my beloved, and his desire is for me" (Song 7:10 NIV 2011). He cares for you and those you love beyond telling. You are forever loved.

Worshipping him is our opportunity to love him in response. It is our response to being loved, forgiven, and known. It is our chance to offer our thanks for being seen, chosen, wanted, understood, cherished, and made new! Worship is our response to seeing Jesus as he really is: worthy, beautiful, endlessly good, kind, forgiving, generous, wonderful, and utterly, completely *for* us.

Worship is an intimate encounter with God that changes us by aligning our spirits with truth even when it doesn't *feel* true. We pour ourselves out onto him, and he pours himself into us. It is a divine uneven exchange that ministers to his heart and renews our own.

Our worship of Jesus pushes back the kingdom of darkness and ushers in the kingdom of God. It changes the atmosphere around us so that others can sense, *These were with Jesus.*

Intimate worship is simply telling God how wonderful he is and why. It is pouring out our love onto him like oil. We bring him all that we are as women, even our weariness and sorrow. *Jesus, I give you my weariness. I give you my doubt. I give you my desire to give up. I come with my thirst. I offer you my desire, my gifting, my weakness, my need, my failure, my everything. I give you all that I am, God. I give you my love.* In our loving of Jesus we become increasingly available for him to continue his deep work in us, transforming us into the women we long to be.

Worshipping Jesus enables us to be like Mary of Bethany and to minister to Jesus with our adoration, our tears, and our thankful hearts. Why don't you take a few minutes and come before him now? Imagine you are sitting at his feet and listening, or washing his feet with your tears, or gazing up at him on the cross, or even bowing before the very much alive and risen Lord. There is no doing this wrong. It makes God so happy when we pause in the midst of our day or create an extended time alone with him, simply to adore him!

Jesus is worthy of our devotion and our thanks. Your Jesus is the One who rode into the depths of the darkest, most dangerous dungeon to rescue his true love. He is the One who will ride again on a white steed with fire in his eyes and a flaming sword in his hand. He has inscribed you into the palm of his nail-pierced hand. He knows your every thought, numbers your every hair, and cherishes your every tear. Jesus weeps for you and with you, longs for you, hopes for you, dreams of you, and rejoices over you with singing. He is the One who has battled all the forces of hell to free you and who battles still.

Jesus is your knight in shining armor. He is the love you have been longing for. He is your dream come true. He is your hero. He is Aslan, the Lion of Judah, and the Lamb of God. He is the Prince of Peace, the Alpha and Omega, the First and the Last, the King of Kings and the Lord of Lords, the Mighty One.

His name is like a kiss and an earthquake. His gaze is on you. He has pledged his love to you and betrothed you to him forever. He is unchangeable, and his love will never fail you.

How will you respond? Love him. Adore him. Worship him.

God is inviting us to become a Mary. He is drawing us to become a woman like Mary, Jesus's mother, a woman of profound, unshakable faith. He is calling us to become a woman like Mary Magdalene, a woman who offered him everything. And Jesus is asking us to become a woman like Mary of Bethany, who knew that our greatest treasure is Jesus and his greatest pleasure is our worship.

13

becoming our true name

I love a good fairy tale. Give me a "happily ever after" any day of the week. Glass slippers, the power of love's first kiss, good triumphing over evil, and everyone's true nature being revealed (She's a dragon! She's a princess!) all make my heart glad. So naturally, the royal wedding of Prince William and Kate Middleton captured my imagination. It was a fairy-tale wedding played out before the world.

An estimated two billion people across the earth watched the nuptials of Will and Kate. It seems the whole world was mesmerized. Lovely Kate was born a "commoner," but now she is married to the future king of England. *People* magazine published a special issue that trumpeted on the cover, "Love Reigns!" Yes! In some deep place, we all long for transcendence; we long for fairy tales to be true!

I well remember the previous royal wedding when the lovely Lady Diana married Charles, the Prince of Wales. My family stayed up past midnight, glued to our little screen, watching as beautiful Diana emerged from the carriage in billowing yards of white. It was a wedding of such pomp and pageantry. We ate it up. So when it came time for the wedding of their son (Prince William), the world was again riveted. Catherine's grace. The maid of honor's behind. The groom's smile, so reminiscent of his mother's.

stolen identity

The heir to the British throne has been given the title "Prince of Wales" since the 1200s when King Edward (remember Longshanks from *Braveheart*? That's the one) conquered the wild and noble Welsh and took from them their land, their laws, and their language. Although he and those after him couldn't quite do it. Eight hundred years later, the language, the unique history, and the flavor of Wales remain.

I confess I have a bit of a crush on Llewellyn the Great. This Prince of Wales was the first to truly unite the country. Much of his life is a picture of Jesus to me, and I don't know why Hollywood has not figured out the glorious story there and made a movie about him, but they should. (Have your people call my people!)

Anyway, he was a nobleman whose grandson and namesake—known as Llewellyn the Last—followed in his grandfather's footsteps and tried to unite, lead, and protect Wales. His life is a noble story as well, but a sad one. He was killed in a small skirmish and unable to save his country from the English invasion that changed the little country's destiny.

Llewellyn the Last had one heir—a baby girl. She was only months old when Wales fell to the English, but since she was an infant and a female, her fate was not as bad as it would have been had she been a boy. She was captured by Edward's troops, and the king interned her at Sempringham Priory in England for the rest of her life. She eventually became a nun in her thirties and died twenty years later, knowing little of her heritage and speaking none of her language.

Her name was Gwenllian. I don't know how to say it correctly, but no one else ever did either. Not to her. The English couldn't pronounce it, so they simplified it. She was a princess in exile, living in a land ruled by her father's enemy. The ache in her heart for her true home was most likely never understood and certainly never fulfilled. She never left the confines of the nunnery her entire life.

The Welsh have a word for the ache in one's heart for its true home, for the longing that goes deeper than understanding: *hiraeth*. It is a holy word for a holy ache.

Gwenllian lived with that ache. She was meant to reign, but her throne was stolen. She was stripped of her authority and lived her life in captivity, never knowing her true identity, never hearing her true name.

Can you imagine being royalty but being treated like a servant? Can you imagine being the daughter of the true king but being held in low regard and never setting foot in your home country for as long as you live? Can you imagine being destined to reign yet never even hearing your true name? Of course you can. The parallels are astonishing. Truly.

Would it have made a difference for Gwenllian if she had known the truth? Would it have mattered in her life, in her heart, if she had known who her father was? Who she was? Does it make a difference in ours? Oh, yes. It makes all the difference in the world.

Let us then remember who we truly are. Let us go further up and further in to all the riches and the joy and the intimacy and the healing that God has for us! Do you remember who you are? Whose you are?

First, you are the daughter of the King. You are your Father's delight. You are the apple of his eye and the one on whom his affections rest.

Second, you are the bride of Christ. You are engaged to the High Prince. You are the beloved of Jesus. There is a royal wedding coming, unparalleled in the history of men and angels, and all the eyes of creation will be riveted and rejoicing.

Third, you are the ally-friend of Jesus, sent to this earth to bring about the invasion by his kingdom. You have a role in a mighty story filled with beauty and danger.

When we believe something is true, it affects the choices we make. We believe gravity exists, so we jump up, safe in the knowledge that we will come down again. We believe the sun will rise, so we go to bed without the fear that night will last forever. But sometimes—actually quite often—God calls us to believe something before we experientially know it. The popular saying is "seeing is believing," but in Christ, believing leads to seeing. God invites us to believe we are who he says we are. Regardless of our experience.

Between sessions of a retreat I was teaching at last year, I met a lovely young woman who approached to ask me to sign her copy of my book *Captivating*. She had a light in her eyes, a vulnerability and a hope and a desire to believe that all I had spoken was true, but also an unbelief. She struggled with her weight. I know the ramifications of being overweight in a world that seems to esteem outward beauty above all other qualities. I know a little bit about what this has cost her.

She handed me her book and confessed that she had read it at least ten times. Well, she had read chapters 1 through 6 at least ten times. She couldn't seem to get past chapter 7. When she would reach chapter 7 she'd feel paralyzed and go back to the beginning.

"What is chapter 7?" I asked.

She opened her book to the chapter and showed me the title: "Romanced." Oh. Now I understood. There was a story here. One that included wounds and messages regarding her being worthy of pursuit, of being wanted.

"What's your name?" I asked.

"Christina," she replied.

I knew that Christina means "follower of Christ," so I asked, "What's your middle name?"

"Louise," she answered. "Do you know what Louise means?"

I didn't. I was curious.

"It means famous warrior!"

Okay then. Pair "follower of Christ" with "famous warrior," and you get one mighty woman of God. That night I had shown a scene from the film *The Fellowship of the Ring* where fair Arwen rides in to save the day. She is strong and beautiful and merciful and filled with grace. She is also the favored daughter of the ruler of the land and the beloved of the true king.

I took another look at Christina and saw her more clearly. "Hello, Arwen," I said.

She gasped! She bubbled over with excitement and told me how much she loved that scene! A new light came into her eyes as she said, "I want to be her!"

I simply repeated myself, "Hello, Arwen." I could see her eyes take in the meaning of my words. I witnessed the flicker of belief, the flame of faith being fanned.

"My parents got it right?"

"You think your parents named you. God named you. He knows who you really are. He knows who you are meant to be."

"Huh," she said and wandered off. At the end of the weekend retreat, she came up to me again, this time clear eyed and steady. She simply said, "I got it."

what's in a name?

What you name something is immeasurably important. Kate Middleton no longer goes by Kate but by Catherine. It's a significant choice. Kate is one of my favorite names, but Catherine is seen as more dignified, more appropriate to royalty.

What's your name? What names do you go by to those who love you?

What names do you call yourself? What do you say to yourself when you pass a mirror? What do you tell yourself about your post-nursing body or your perimenopausal tummy or your memory that so often seems to be slipping away? What words do you use?

There is power in what we name ourselves. There is power in what other people name us as well. Both the power to bless and the power to curse come from the heart and flows out of the mouth through words. What we call something, what we are called, whether good or evil, will play itself out in our lives:

> More than 200 Indian girls whose names mean "unwanted" in Hindi chose new names Saturday for a fresh start in life.
>
> A central Indian district held a renaming ceremony it hopes will give the girls new dignity and help fight wide-spread gender discrimination that gives India a skewed gender ratio, with far more boys than girls.
>
> The girls—wearing their best outfits with barrettes, braids and bows in their hair—lined up to receive certificates with their new names along with small flower bouquets from Satara district officials in Maharashtra state.
>
> In shedding names like "Nakusa" or "Nakushi," which mean "unwanted" in Hindi, some girls chose to name themselves after Bollywood stars like "Aishwarya" … Some just wanted traditional names with happier meanings, such as "Vaishali" or "prosperous, beautiful and good."
>
> "Now in school, my classmates and friends will be calling me this new name, and that makes me very happy," said a 15-year-old girl who had been named Nakusa by a grandfather disappointed by her birth.[1]

Isn't that beautiful? And horrible? And vitally important?

What you call someone or something is powerful. It affects your life, your relationships, and your walk with God. What you call yourself *affects your ability to become who you are meant to be.* God knows there is power in what we call ourselves. Knowing this, listen to the fierce intention of God, who says he will change *your* name:

> Because I love Zion [this means the people of God;
>> put your name in here: "Because I love Julie;
>> because I love Sue"],
>> I will not keep still.
> Because my heart yearns for [her],
>> I cannot remain silent.
> I will not stop praying for her
>> until her righteousness shines like the dawn,
>> and her salvation blazes like a burning torch.
> The nations will see your righteousness.
>> World leaders will be blinded by your glory.
> And you will be given a new name
>> by the LORD's own mouth.
> The LORD will hold you in his hand for all to see—
>> a splendid crown in the hand of God.
> Never again will you be called "The Forsaken City"
>> or "The Desolate Land."
> Your new name will be "The City of God's Delight"
>> and "The Bride of God,"
> for the LORD delights in you
>> and will claim you as his bride. (Isa. 62:1–4 NLT)

This beautiful passage comes after Isaiah 61, which promises your healing and restoration, your deliverance also from the Enemy. Now God promises a new name. No longer will you be called Deserted but Sought After. You are not unwanted. You are Pursued. You are worth pursuing, chasing after, romancing. You are wanted.

God wants us to name things correctly, including ourselves. It's vitally important that we do.

> I belong to my beloved,
>   and his desire is for me. (Song 7:10 NIV 2011)

God names you "beloved." What does beloved mean? It means one greatly loved, dear to the heart. It means admired, adored, cherished, darling. Beloved means dear, dear one, dear*est*, esteemed, favorite, honey. It means ladylove, light of love, loved one, lover, precious, prized, respected, and revered. Beloved means you. It means who you are to him. And who you are to him means everything.

God calls you to believe it.

The fruit of knowing who you are to Christ is intimacy with him. It isn't walking around all puffed up. *Oh, look at me! I'm something special!* The fruit is neither pride nor arrogance. The fruit is humility. It is surrendered gratefulness. The fruit of believing we are *who God says we are* is a deepening love for Jesus. We love because he first loved us. Belief evokes a response; we choose to draw near to this God who prizes us. And that is exactly what God is after.

So who are you?

Well, you may be like me, and it's hard for me to answer this question with grace when I just got so irritated with my husband that I had to leave the room. God sees me as lovely, but lovely thoughts have not been filling my mind just now. I need help! When we believe that our truest identity is a sinner, then we walk around ashamed, accused, condemned. Separated from God. Which does not make for a happy camper and which is exactly where our Enemy, the Devil, wants us to live. The Devil is called the accuser of the brethren for a reason.

Hang on a sec; I need to go apologize to my husband …

Okay, I'm back. When the focus of our heart is solely on our failings, then our heart spirals down. God tells us not to focus on our failings but on his faithfulness. He calls us to gaze not on our brokenness but on our Healer. He says, "Let us fix our eyes on Jesus, the author and perfecter of our faith" (Heb. 12:2). We move toward what we focus on.

We are warned in Scripture to not think more highly of ourselves than we ought, but honestly that is a rare woman. I have yet to meet that woman. But I have met a lot of women who think much less of themselves than they ought. Certainly much less than God does. And that is not only disheartening, it is dangerous. Why? Because you cannot live well, you cannot love well, and you cannot fulfill your destiny if you do not know who you are.

You cannot become yourself if you do not know who you are to become.

scoreboard

My friend's son Gannon is a superb soccer player. As a freshman in high school he helped lead the varsity team to the state championship. He is a quiet, polite young man who transforms into a warrior once he hits the field. During one of his recent games, he had an opportunity to believe.

Gannon's team was in the lead by three goals, a massive lead in soccer. Guarding him was a player who used insults to try to keep Gannon from being his glorious soccer-playing self. They call it "talking smack." His was incessant. Mean. "You are the worst player on this team." "You can't even kick the ball." "No one on your team likes you." "You shouldn't be on this team." "You're just a baby freshman." "Go home, little boy."

Sound familiar? You're blowing it. You can't do this well at all. You never will. You're not qualified. You don't have any real friends. You should just go home.

What do you hear when you forget a friend's birthday? Leave a party? Sin?

Gannon's accuser didn't take a break. He started right in again after any time out. Gannon said it was the most difficult thing he had ever endured on the field. "You missed! You are always going to miss." Accusations hurt. Spiritual warfare hurts.

Gannon didn't engage him in a verbal battle. He didn't entertain the accusations coming against him or defend himself. He merely answered him, "Scoreboard." That is all he ever replied. "Scoreboard." His accuser could say what he wanted; there was no silencing him. But Gannon's team was winning the game. He and his teammates were playing well. The truth lay in the scoreboard. Gannon's defense lay in the truth. There was no catching them. You bet they won that game. Now that silenced his accuser.

Scoreboard. Done and done. Jesus has won our victory, and we are victorious as well, in him. We are not defined by our sin, our failures, or our past. We are forever and only defined by the finished work of Jesus Christ. Everything Jesus did and won was for us. We were slaves to sin, yes. But because of Jesus, we are slaves no longer. We are daughters. We are brides.

> *Watch your thoughts for they become words. Watch your words for*
> *they become actions. Watch your actions for they become habits.*
> *Watch your habits, for they become your character. And watch your*
> *character, for it becomes your destiny! What we think, we become.*
> —Author Unknown

What we think, we become.

In the midst of your day—in the mess, the mundane, the glorious—when you laugh and live well and when you don't, get into the habit of stopping and asking yourself, "What am I thinking is true about myself?" If it does not line up with the Word of God, reject it as a lie. Replace it with the truth.

What would it be like right now to entertain the possibility in your heart that all God says about you is true?

You are his delight.

You make him happy just by being you.

He thinks you're lovely.

You are his beloved.

You are the one who has captured his heart.

What difference would it make in your life if it really were true? Think of it. Let your heart go there a moment. Because it does make all the difference in the world.

You must ask him. *Am I your beloved? How do you see me? Do you delight in me? Do you love me because you're God and that's your job, or do you love me simply for me?*

You, dear heart, you *are* the beloved.

> *Jesus, thank you for this truth about me. I receive it. I agree with you, and I declare that I am your daughter. I am chosen, holy, and dearly loved. I am the apple of your eye. I am your beloved, and your desire is for me. Please, write this truth deeply in my heart. In Jesus's Name, I pray. Amen.*

who will you become?

Have you ever had to go to an event that you didn't want to go to, a party or a baby shower where you knew no one except the guest of honor? I had one I needed to attend recently, and I wasn't very happy about it. I complained to my husband that I had to go and spend hours with people I had never met nor would ever see again. Blah blah blah. And John said, "Rename it. Call it good." Riiiigghht—it's not evil, it's good. It's an opportunity to bless someone I care very much about. It's a chance to celebrate her life. I renamed it, changed my frame of reference, and went with a happy heart.

There are many things we need to rename in our lives. Our work. Our relationships. Even our life itself. Rename them. Rename your life. It's good. Because your life belongs to our good God, and he's got you. Rename yourself. God has.

My parents named me Stasi. It means resurrection. There is a lot in my life that has needed resurrecting over the years—my wounded heart, my damaged sexuality, my broken self-perception, my dreams, my relationships, my calling. And God *is* resurrecting every area of my life to *life*. He is resurrecting my mind to be able to believe that all he has made, and all he has made *me*, is good. He is resurrecting my dreams and my desires and even my yearning to be deeply known and perfectly loved. Yes, my parents named me Stasi, but really it was God who named me "Resurrection."

Do you know what your given name means? It's a good idea to find out. And if you don't like the meaning you initially discover, press in to find out more about it. Ask God to reveal to you *why* he named you what he did. A friend of mine's name is Melanie. I asked her what it means, and with a little shrug she told me, "It means dark." Huh. Dark. We pressed in to find out more about what her name means and discovered it doesn't mean simply "dark." It means "dark beauty." In Hebrew it actually means "Grace-filled beauty." Song of Songs says, "Dark am I, yet lovely." Which can mean, "Yes, I am imperfect, and I see my many failings and sins, but when God looks at me, he sees my beauty, not my sin. To Jesus, I am and have only ever been lovely." That's what Melanie means. See, it's a good idea to find out.

Because whatever else is true about what you are named, God says:

No longer are you called Desolate, but Married.

No longer are you alone or unseen; your name is Sought After, Beloved. Mine.

No longer are you called Nakusa, Unwanted.

Your name is Vaishali—Prosperous, Beautiful, and Good.

As women growing in our own becoming, we want to live with holy intention. We want to be awake to the present moment, those around us, the Spirit within us, and our own souls. We are meant to live lives of significance. It is right that we desire to live for a purpose higher than protecting our skin from sun damage and being well liked. We want to live unto a high calling, a meaningful purpose, and that purpose flows out of our identity.

Knowing who we are enables us to live the life we have been born to live—the life the seen and unseen world needs us to live. We need to know who we are and own who we are. Who *are* you? What is your identity—*really*?

You are a new creation in Christ, more than a conqueror. Victorious. Strong. Empowered. Safe. Secure. Sealed. You are a channel of the life and love of God. You are alive in Christ. You are the beloved of God. You are his.

Who is Jesus? He is the love you have been looking for all your life, and he has never taken his eyes off of you. He has a name for you that he wants you to fully become; he holds your true identity, and this is what you are meant to grow into. So you'll want to ask Jesus your true name (or names—he often has several for us).

Jesus, I choose to believe that I am your beloved and that your desire is for me. I choose to believe that I am no longer forsaken or deserted, but that I am your Delight, sought after and dearly loved. Jesus, I want to become the woman you

*have in mind for me to be. Show me who she is; show me who
I really am, who I was always meant to be. Tell me my true
name; give me an image of who you see me becoming. Give
me eyes to see and ears to hear and the courage to accept what
you are saying. Tell me, Jesus.*

And as he does, dear one, choose to believe.

> You will be called by a new name
> that the mouth of the LORD will bestow. (Isa. 62:2)

14

take heart

It takes courage to grow up and become who you really are.

—e.e. cummings

Julie's dreams are finally coming true.

She thought she'd be married a long time ago. Keeping her hope alive and continuing to trust God with her desires had proven to be quite the difficult task. Through years of aching, Julie's soul had been crafted into a display of splendor in the hand of her God. As she continued to seek after Jesus in holy and sometimes circuitous pursuit, he did not assuage her desire for marriage but deepened it. Some days, some months, it seemed too much to bear. Julie's heart is a beautiful one. Her journey into becoming her truer self is not a straight one. The wonder of God's unfolding story of her life is a holy one. Julie chose to stay awake to her desire and alive to her sometimes doubt-filled heart, and in his perfect timing (which often seems a tad bit late), God brought her man.

Since then, Julie has discovered that though her husband is the love of her life, the truest gift came through knowing Jesus more deeply in the tending of her heart. Jesus remains the Love (capital L) of Julie's life. Because of that, she is safe to become her true self, and in that she is loving her husband well. She recently wrote: "I am more myself than I have ever been, and I am so happy."

Of course. The two go hand in hand.

We will never be happy as long as we are trying to live apart from ourselves or in disregard of ourselves, our hearts, our desires, our ache. Though happiness is never the highest goal, it comes to us naturally when the other aspects of our lives are in order. "Seek ye first the kingdom of God, and his righteousness; and all these things shall be added unto you" (Matt. 6:33 KJV).

Love is always the highest goal. Love of God, of others, and of ourselves: the woman God has created us to be. We don't want to live in spite of ourselves, but we want to embrace ourselves, owning the multifaceted mysterious women we are and the unique way we bring Jesus to the world.

You are the only you there has ever been or ever will be.

God made you *you* on purpose. Now. For a reason.

The world does not need yet another woman who despises the lovely creation that she is. God does not long for another woman who rejects herself and, by extension, him. The world needs a woman who is thankful for how God has made her, trusts that he is transforming her, and actually enjoys who she is. It's a good thing to like who you are. God likes you! We get to like ourselves too! When you like yourself, you are free to enjoy others, and in your presence people experience an invitation to become and enjoy who they truly are as well.

Life begets life. Joy begets joy. Becoming begets becoming.

Be who God meant you to be and you will set the world on fire.

—St. Catherine of Siena

when we haven't the strength

The Broadmoor Hotel is a five-star luxury resort that sits at the base of Pikes Peak with a lovely lake at its center and, yes, swans floating on that lake. The Broadmoor is elegant, old, and expensive. And I was going there for dinner. What to wear?

I wasn't going for a romantic dinner with my husband but to a work-related one. It was to be a gathering of about twenty-five people whom my husband either worked with or for and whom I very much wanted to impress. I was going to need to sit up straight and mind my manners. I was nervous.

The dinner was held in a small room on the very top floor off the Penrose Room, about as classy as Colorado can get. A long table was in the center of the room, and as John and I arrived, people began to take their seats. Waiters stood at the ready. Two empty chairs remained on either side at the end of the table, right next to the highest-ranking person in the room. *My mother taught me how to behave. I can do this!* I told myself.

Greetings were exchanged, and then I sat down. Instantly, the beautifully carved chair broke under my weight. Loudly. Cruelly. Miraculously, I caught myself before sprawling on the ground on top of the splintered wood. Waiters were there in a moment, apologizing profusely for the faulty chair and making sure I was all right.

What a beginning.

Somehow, I managed to not slide completely into the abyss of shame and stayed somewhat present in the evening and with the people around me. I tried to be lively, engaging, and funny, hiding how mortified I was with conversation. (But with such an inauspicious start, I will tell you that the evening did not go well. Chair or no chair, we never supped with that group again.)

People often hide their embarrassment behind humor. The chubby girl becomes the funny girl. The darling with the bad skin is very good at sports, and the skinny one who is never asked to a dance excels in her courses.

Sometimes we need to hide. Sometimes bearing the weight of the sorrow in the moment would prevent us from being able to take our next breath. But hiding simply keeps us hidden. Our hearts, when buried beneath shame and dashed hopes, cannot rise, and Cinderella never gets out of the cinders. To be women who are alive and engaged with their world, we cannot remain hidden, but sometimes we just don't possess the strength to push out of the cellar by ourselves.

The wonderful thing is, we are not by ourselves. Ever.

"Never will I leave you, never will I forsake you" (Heb. 13:5) is a promise of faithful relationship from a faithful God who has never and will never leave us on our own. Jesus held my embarrassed heart as I stood there waiting for a new (and hopefully stronger) chair to be brought to me. He stands today between me and the endless accusations coming my way. He fights for me. He fights for you. In the game of hide-and-seek, he is ever and always the Seeker. In the wounding of life, he is always the Healer.

For me to continue on the journey of becoming myself, I need him to find me where I am still hiding. I need him to strengthen me when I am too weak to believe. I need him to kiss me awake in the places of my heart where I remain asleep. I need him to breathe his fiery love into the chambers within that are frozen by fear. I need him to hold my hope and tend my heart and tell me once again who I am. I cannot do this alone, and neither can you.

Thank goodness we are not alone.

> God is within her, she will not fall;
> God will help her at break of day. (Ps. 46:5)

receiving a vision of yourself

About twenty years ago, I was at church and in a very low place. I felt hideously ugly. I was telling myself that I looked like Jabba the Hutt. (Not very nice words to say to oneself—remember the power of naming things.) Kneeling in prayer, I asked God, "How do you see me?" In my sanctified imagination, I immediately saw a woman kneeling. The sun filtering through the window framed her in a golden beam of light. She was wearing a lovely fitted white satin dress. Her hair was softly yet ornately done up with seed pearls in it. She was beautiful, a bride clearly held in the gaze of her God.

He saw me then as beautiful. He sees me now as beautiful.

When God looks at his daughter—me, you, any beloved one—he does not view her through the veil of her sin, the shroud of her failures, or the canopy of her past. When God looks at us, he sees us through the blood of Jesus. When God looks at you, he sees the righteousness of Jesus Christ. You are a spotless, pure, stunning bride. Oh, how we need to see ourselves as he does! Both who we are in this moment and the woman he is forming in us.

> *We need to ask God for a more radiant picture of Him*
> *and a more brilliant picture of ourselves.*
> —Graham Cooke

Who do you think you are? Who are you on the road to becoming? Do you have a vision of who you could become? How does God see you? What is his vision of who you are to become? It's vital that we ask him that question. And then wait for his answer.

Having a vision of who you are becoming informs your present. We live today knowing who we are going to be tomorrow. Knowing who you are becoming puts hope in your heart and a spring in your step. The key is to *choose to believe* we are who God says we are. And then rest in the knowledge that God is the one responsible for our transformation. We lean into him. We will fail. He will not.

So ask him. *How do you see me, God? Please give me your vision of the woman I am to become.* And then write it down. Write down what you hear from God or merely what, by faith, you choose to believe is becoming true for you because you want it.

Here is something I wrote in my journal in 2007:

> The woman I am becoming is strong, powerful, sure, unwavering, kind, honest, loving, generous, and wise. I am not waylaid by others' false expectations and demands because I know I am the Beloved of God and I know what I am to be about. I am a Worshipper. Wife. Mother. Friend. Prayer Warrior. Truth Teller. Writer. Conference Speaker. And that is awesome and enough.
>
> I don't have to question or prove my value or worth because God has proven my worth and says I am priceless, precious, and invaluable … every moment of every single day.
>
> The woman I am becoming is not bound to food or any other false god or false comforter. I am free of shame. I am healthy, beautiful, fresh, and happy. I have energy. My heart is centered in the heart of God. I love my life, and I like who I am.
>
> There is power released when I pray because I pray the will of God, wielding my God-given authority in Christ. I do the work God ordained for me to do—setting people free from bondage and darkness and releasing hearts to the love of God. I bring Jesus's healing. I am a merciful, lovely, Holy Spirit–filled woman who laughs freely and often.

I am not that woman fully. Yet. But I *am* becoming that woman. I am more her now than I was in 2007 when I wrote this. Writing it down helped me embrace the vision, accept it, believe it, and move toward it. Who are you becoming?

To become our true selves will require not only that we trust God more deeply but also that we are willing to take what we may feel are enormous risks. We will need to risk believing that what God has said about us is *true*.

We must risk being more beautiful, more powerful, more loved, more loving, more involved, more intimate, more connected, more glorious, and more gifted than we thought we ever could be.

We must risk believing we are worth loving, fighting for, protecting, and cherishing. God has revealed the truth to us through his Word. You want to know what he thinks about you? Open up the Bible. Camp out in Ephesians 1 for a few months! God has revealed himself to us through his Son, Jesus Christ. Want to know what God is like? Look at Jesus. He is the face of God. (To know what Jesus is really like, read *Beautiful Outlaw*. I cannot recommend it strongly enough!)

God has revealed himself to us and ourselves to us. Now we must flex our muscles of faith and choose to believe him in the moments when we are experiencing it and when we are not.

Becoming ourselves requires standing against the world's current— the demands, the expectations, the assault of daily realities, and our own histories. We cannot afford to indulge in our inner diatribes any longer. To become true ourselves will require that we speak the truth in love, even to ourselves.

courage

Promise me you'll always remember—you're braver than you believe, and stronger than you seem, and smarter than you think.

—Christopher Robin to Pooh

To risk anything requires that we possess the courage to risk it. Jesus says, "In this world, you will have trouble. But take heart! I have overcome the world" (John 16:33). Some versions translate "take heart" as "be of good courage." Courage is from the Old French word *cor*, meaning "heart." Take heart. Have courage. "Because of me," Jesus said, "you can do this."

Jesus knows that continuing to become ourselves will take mighty courage! There is a reason we shrank back years ago from our hearts, from love, from our dreams, from our vulnerability. But, friend, the days of shrinking back need to be over. With mercy in his eyes, God calls us to be women of courage:

> Have I not commanded you? Be strong and courageous.
> Do not be afraid; do not be discouraged, for the LORD
> your God will be with you wherever you go. (Josh. 1:9
> NIV 2011)

> Do not let your hearts be troubled and do not be afraid.
> (John 14:27)

> Do not give way to fear. (1 Peter 3:6)

> Be on your guard; stand firm in the faith; be courageous;
> be strong. (1 Cor. 16:13 NIV 2011)

We live in a world filled with beauty and wonder, adventure and laughter, but also too often filled with difficulty, fear, danger, and pain. Courage is the quality of spirit that enables one to face danger, pain, difficulty, or fear with *confidence*. We can have confidence! Not based on our own ability to manage life but based on the faithfulness of Jesus.

Confidence is from the Latin words *con* and *fide*, which mean "with faith." Our confidence rests in the strength and goodness of God. Living a life of courage is not about striving to become something or someone else. It is resting by faith in the God who says, *I have called you, and I will do it!* (1 Thess. 5:24).

To become ourselves, we let ourselves be immersed in the love of God. Drink from his mercy. Live in his grace. See ourselves through his eyes. Receiving his life is the only way for us to live the life we all so long to live. On our own, we simply can't pull this life off. I can find my way to the freeway, but I can't find my way to freedom. I can barely pull off an evening; forget about a lifetime. So what is the big secret to living with courage and becoming the woman God created you to be? I'll tell you.

The secret is you can't. *You* can't. But Jesus can. Christ in you can. He is the secret! There is nothing that makes God tremble. Jesus who died on the cross for you entered into the worst nightmare imaginable and demanded that Satan hand over the keys to hell. Jesus rose triumphantly and is seated at the right hand of God. This same Jesus:

> Calmed the storm and walked on the water
> Healed the leper and fed the thousands
> Gave sight to the blind, hearing to the deaf, and life to
>   the dead
> Cleared the temple and received the children
> Rebuked the Pharisees, forgave sinners, and cast out
>   demons

And he is still doing it. Jesus is alive today and living his life *through you*. Remember, "I have been crucified with Christ and I no longer live, but Christ lives in me" (Gal. 2:20). Paul says the whole mystery of the gospel comes down to this: "Christ in you, the hope of glory" (Col. 1:27).

Christ is your life and your breath and your hope and your courage. In him you live and breathe and have your being. And apart from him, you can do nothing (John 15:5). But once you have accepted Jesus as your Lord and Savior, received his death in your place, received his forgiveness for your sins, invited him to take his rightful place and rule your heart, you will never be apart from Christ again.

You are in the palm of his hand, and nothing can take you out. That's the secret to becoming ourselves! We increasingly lean on Jesus, calling on him to live his life through us. And as he does, we are transformed into the very image of God. We discover the brilliant truth that *the more his we become, the more ourselves we become.*

The more we know Jesus as he really is, the more we love him. The more we love him, the more our lives are transformed. You are beautiful, and your beauty is increasing. It's growing. Really! We are courageous women of God and becoming more so!

He is the one who gives us the confidence to become. He will give you courage as he lives his life through you. He will give you the courage:

> To press in to God
> To believe
> To keep your heart alive
> To trust him in the face of immense brokenness and
>   suffering in the world
> To face your fears and ask for healing again

He will give you the courage:

> To answer the phone
> To walk into the room
> To have the conversation

To stand up against injustice

To get back up

To believe that what he says about us is true: we are not
defined by our addictions, our sins, our failures, our
histories, or other peoples' opinions

To know he is Love

Most messages for women take a wrong turn in one of two directions. However subtle they may try to be, one style of message is always some version of *Get Your Act Together*. Be more disciplined, more faithful, more humble, more whatever. All the pressure winds up back on us. But no, no, *no*! Jesus is your life, your strength, your healer; it is the life of Jesus in you, restoring you, that allows you to live as the woman you were made to be. He is your courage.

The other camp takes the direction of *It Isn't About You*. Just serve, just obey God, just set your desires aside, because that's what holy women do. It can sound biblical because it exalts Jesus, but it ends up crushing women. He made *you* on purpose; he is fully committed to restoring *you*. Of course you matter—what did Jesus die for if not *you*? This journey we are on isn't about tossing ourselves into a ditch in the name of holiness; it is about becoming the woman God made us to be.

What we look at, we move toward. When you are learning to drive a car, you are told, "Keep your eyes on the road!" Likewise, when you are riding a horse, the direction you are looking is the direction the horse will take you. What you are looking at becomes what you are aiming at. It is the same with our thought life. Our transformation takes the form of what has captured our attention.

Our attention becomes our intention.

And I know it can be really hard sometimes, this life of ours. Days come when I just want to crawl back into bed and pull the covers up over my head. I want to disconnect my phone and take a break from my life. And there are days when I do just that. For a bit. That's actually a good thing. There are seasons when I need to retreat so that afterward I can advance.

Now I know that if I don't want to get out of bed for a week and I'm not sick, there's something else going on inside that needs attending to. But every now and again, pulling away to tend our weary hearts and bodies is necessary. We are not in a sprint here. Our lives are a marathon, and in order to run the race set before us, we're going to need to pace ourselves. The only possible way to live is to keep our gaze on Jesus, depend on him, follow him, and have him carry us and all that we carry.

Sometimes life is ruthlessly painful, but Jesus tells us to press on. Hebrews 10:39 says, "We do not belong to those who shrink back" (NIV 2011). Yes, we may need to retreat for a bit, but by the grace of God, we will not shrink back. We will continue moving forward, bringing the kingdom of God to bear on the desperate world around us and becoming ever more our true selves.

Dear one, you will not be able to do it perfectly. But Jesus has and will. Because of Jesus, you can fight well. Plan well. Pray well. Listen well. Live well. Serve well. Love well. Become well. One day, Christ will tell you your story, and you will be amazed at the glory, the beauty, the redemption, and the presence of Jesus throughout your life in ways you can't even now imagine.

My twelve-year-old friend Delaney has painted my toenails green. They are, besides my heart, the youngest thing about me. I point them up at the clear Colorado sky as I prop my feet on the rail and lean back in my chair. I am drinking in the beauty of a summer in full bloom. I feel so happy. A laugh rises up from my belly, and I let it loose, knowing that truly I can, like the woman in Proverbs 31, laugh at the future. I know winter will come again. And again. I know that there are seasons ahead for me when the landscape of my soul may freeze once more and appear dead. But

I am not afraid of what is to come. I have read the last chapter of the Book. I know that Jesus has won the victory. My victory. I know that he has come for me and continues to come for me and that when my story is told, I will be smiling.

He beckons me onward. He beckons me upward. I've answered him yes. I will have a thousand opportunities to answer him yes again this very month. So will you.

Come on, my sister. Let's go together. Let's press on to the goal that is set before us—to become fully transformed, fully alive, fully ourselves, fully his.

To him who is able to keep you from falling and to present you before his glorious presence without fault and with great joy—to the only God our Savior be glory, majesty, power and authority, through Jesus Christ our Lord, before all ages, now and forevermore! Amen. (Jude vv. 24–25)

afterword

I think it's just a bit funny that this is called the "Afterword." Let me be clear—it doesn't mean, "after you've become yourself," but simply, "after you've read the book." Remember, it's a journey! We *will* arrive one day and be fully ourselves, fully restored, and fully transformed. But for now—let the process continue!

I want to encourage you to stay with it. This isn't the kind of book that you read and then simply toss aside for the next thing. This is the journey of your life. Your growing in knowing God is the key to your living the life you are meant to live. Let the messages and themes in this book marinate in your heart. There is more life to be had. There is more healing, more freedom, and more joy! Here are some helps we have created for you:

The *Becoming Myself Study Guide*—for use in groups or as individuals.

A *Becoming Myself* video series—releasing in January 2014! Perfect for groups! (The study guide can be used with the book alone or with the video series.)

Facebook—come to my Stasi Eldredge page! I'll be posting blogs and videos and just sharing life with you.

Ransomed Heart—our ministry is a treasure trove of resources. We're a little band devoted to Jesus, to bringing his kingdom and to restoring the hearts of men and women all over the world. We have so many resources to help you grow in your own becoming! Come visit us at www.ransomedheart.com. Sign up to receive the free (!) Daily Readings. Browse our store. Come to one of our conferences. "Like" us on Facebook. Read our blogs. Join with others who are on this path. Our desire is to strengthen the hearts of God's people. We want to introduce Jesus to folks who've never met him or who have a lower version of who he really is!

The more we know Jesus, the more we love him. The more we love him, the more healed and ourselves we become. People actually will ask you for the reason for the hope that is within you! Jesus is the reason. He is so marvelous, and there is no end to discovering the beauty and majesty of his alluring heart. So let the adventure continue.

We're in it together!

With and in and for Christ,
Stasi

the daily prayer

Over the years, we've learned a great deal about prayer—mostly through facing our own trials, crying out for help, studying the Scripture, and asking Jesus, as the disciples did, "Teach us to pray!" We offer to you "The Daily Prayer"—the prayer we have found to be so effective that we don't let a day go by now without praying some version of it. May it bring you freedom, restoration, breakthrough, and life!

> My dear Lord Jesus, I come to you now to be restored in you, to be renewed in you, to receive your life and your love and all the grace and mercy I so desperately need this day. I honor you as my Lord, and I surrender every aspect and dimension of my life to you. I give you my spirit, soul, and body, my heart, mind, and will. I cover myself with your blood—my spirit, soul, and body, my heart, mind, and will. I ask your Holy Spirit to restore me in you, renew me in you, and lead this time of prayer. In all that I now pray, I stand in total agreement with your Spirit and with all those praying

for me by the Spirit of God and by the Spirit of God alone.

Dearest God, holy and victorious Trinity, you alone are worthy of all my worship, my heart's devotion, all my praise, all my trust, and all the glory of my life. I love you, I worship you, and I give myself over to you in my heart's search for life. You alone are Life, and you have become my life. I renounce all other gods, every idol, and I give to you, God, the place in my heart and in my life that you truly deserve. This is all about you and not about me. You are the Hero of this story, and I belong to you. I ask your forgiveness for my every sin. Search me, know me, reveal to me where you are working in my life, and grant to me the grace of your healing and deliverance and a deep and true repentance.

Heavenly Father, thank you for loving me and choosing me before you made the world. You are my true Father—my Creator, Redeemer, Sustainer, and the True End of all things, including my life. I love you; I trust you; I worship you. I give myself over to you, Father, to be one with you as Jesus is one with you. Thank you for proving your love for me by sending Jesus. I receive him and all his life and all his work, which you ordained for me. Thank you for including me in Christ, forgiving me my sins, granting me his righteousness, making me complete in him. Thank you for making me alive with Christ, raising me with him, seating me with him at your right hand, establishing me in his authority, and anointing me with your love and your Spirit and your favor. I receive it all with thanks and give it total claim to my life—my spirit, soul, and body, my heart, mind, and will.

Jesus, thank you for coming to ransom me with your own life. I love you, worship you, trust you. I give myself over to you, to be one with you in all things. I receive all the work and triumph of your cross, death, blood, and sacrifice for me—through which my every sin is atoned for; I am ransomed, delivered from the kingdom of darkness, and transferred to your kingdom; my sin nature is removed; my heart is circumcised unto God; and every claim being made against me is canceled and disarmed. I take my place now in your cross and death, dying with you to sin, to my flesh, to this world, to the Evil One and his kingdom. I take up the cross and crucify my flesh with all its pride, arrogance, unbelief, and idolatry [add anything else you are currently struggling with]. I put off the old man. Apply to me all the work and triumph in your cross, death, blood, and sacrifice; I receive it with thanks and give it total claim to my spirit, soul, and body, my heart, mind, and will.

Jesus, I also receive you as my Life, and I receive all the work and triumph in your resurrection, through which you have conquered sin, death, judgment, and the Evil One. Death has no power over you, nor does any foul thing. And I have been raised with you to a new life, to live your life—dead to sin and alive to God. I take my place now in your resurrection and in your life, and I give my life to you to live your life. I am saved by your life. I reign in life through your life. I receive your hope, love, faith, joy, goodness, trueness, wisdom, power, and strength. Apply to me all the work and triumph in your resurrection; I receive it with thanks, and I give it total claim to my spirit, soul, and body, my heart, mind, and will.

Jesus, I also sincerely receive you as my authority, rule, and dominion, my everlasting victory against Satan and his kingdom, and my ability to bring your kingdom at all times and in every way. I receive all the work and triumph in your ascension, through which Satan has been judged and cast down. All authority in heaven and on earth has been given to you. *All* authority in the heavens and on this earth has been given to you, Jesus, and you are worthy to receive all glory and honor, power and dominion, now and forever. I take my place now in your authority and in your throne, through which I have been raised with you to the right hand of the Father and established in your authority. I give myself to you, to reign with you always. Apply to me all the work and triumph in your authority and your throne; I receive it with thanks, and I give it total claim to my spirit, soul, and body, my heart, mind, and will.

I now bring the authority, rule, and dominion of the Lord Jesus Christ, and the full work of Christ, over my life today—over my home, my household, my work, over all my kingdom and domain. I bring the authority of the Lord Jesus Christ and the full work of Christ against every evil power coming against me—against every foul spirit, every foul power and device. [You might need to name them. What has been attacking you?] I cut them off in the name of the Lord, I bind and banish them from me and from my kingdom now, in the mighty name of Jesus Christ. I also bring the full work of Christ between me and every person, and I allow only the love of God and only the Spirit of God between us.

Holy Spirit, thank you for coming. I love you, I worship you, I trust you. I receive all the work and triumph in Pentecost, through which you have come; clothed me with power from on high; sealed me in Christ; and become my union with the Father and the Son, the Spirit of truth in me, the life of God in me, my Counselor, Comforter, Strength, and Guide. I honor you as Lord, and I fully give to you every aspect and dimension of my spirit, soul, and body, my heart, mind, and will—to be filled with you, to walk in step with you in all things. Fill me afresh, Holy Spirit. Restore my union with the Father and the Son. Lead me into all truth, anoint me for all of my life and walk and calling, and lead me deeper into Jesus today. I receive you with thanks, and I give you total claim to my life.

Heavenly Father, thank you for granting to me every spiritual blessing in Christ Jesus. I claim the riches of Christ Jesus over my life today. I bring the blood of Christ once more over my spirit, soul, and body, over my heart, mind, and will. I put on the full armor of God—the belt of truth, breastplate of righteousness, shoes of the gospel, helmet of salvation; I take up the shield of faith and sword of the Spirit, and I choose to be strong in the Lord and in the strength of your might, to pray at all times in the Spirit.

Jesus, thank you for your angels. I summon them in the name of Jesus Christ and instruct them to destroy all that is raised against me, to establish your kingdom over me, to guard me day and night. I ask you to send forth your Spirit to raise up prayer and intercession for me. I now call forth the kingdom of God throughout my home, my household, my kingdom and domain in the authority of the Lord Jesus Christ, giving all glory and honor and thanks to him. In Jesus's name, amen.

prayer of salvation

If you have never given your life to Jesus Christ, now would be the perfect time. This is the moment he chose for you. Time for you to come home to the heart of God. This prayer will help you:

Jesus, I need you. I need your life and your love. I believe you are the Son of God. I believe that your death on the cross was for me—to rescue me from sin and death and to restore me to the Father. I choose right now to surrender my life to you. I turn from my sin and my self-determination, and I give my life to you. Thank you for loving me and forgiving me. Come and take your rightful place in my heart and in my life. Be my Savior and my Lord. Live in me; live through me. I am yours.

acknowledgments

The beginning of a new calendar year is a natural time for a person to look back, take stock, and give thanks. It turns out that writing an acknowledgement for a book is another one. Where to begin?

Some authors cast a wide net of thanks that include neighbors, childhood friends, and elementary school teachers. Other authors narrow the field, nodding to the fact that every person who has made a significant contribution to their life cannot be listed. At least not here. I choose to follow their example with the sure hope that one day, I will have the opportunity to thank everyone in leisurely depth. I look forward to that day, but in the meantime, I must at least name a few.

My agent, Curtis Yates, believed in this book before I even did. His encouragement, guidance, and faith have been a huge gift to me. Agent extraordinaire, Curtis, thank you for all your skill and hard work. I count you not only an ally but also a friend.

My editor, Karen Lee Thorp, is everything an excellent editor should be. She fine-tuned my writing with her questions, her gentle honing, and her vast experience. I am so grateful.

The entire team at David C Cook is a group of people I am honored, blessed, and privileged to partner with. I am so happy to join you in your mission and pray that with Jesus we are indeed "transforming lives together."

These many years, a great company of saints has surrounded me. Worshippers and warriors who love me gracefully, encourage me deeply, and share the journey with me—Lori, Craig, Carrie, Sue, Sallie, Rie, Julie (x2), Abbey, Susie, Becky, Cherie, Morgan, Lisa, Amanda, Sam, and all the noble team of Ransomed Heart, I thank you, dear friends. I couldn't do it without you. I treasure you.

My sons. Oh, my sons. Sam, Blaine, and Luke, I have learned far more from you than I have taught. You have my heart always.

And then there is my husband. John has loved me, guided me, journeyed with me, and shown me the face of Jesus for more than thirty years. He has been my sounding board for this writing project, and I trust him with my words, my thoughts, my dreams, and most importantly, my heart.

Now to acknowledge my King. He deserves much more than a nod, even much more than a wide blanket of awed thanksgiving. The truth is that every worthy and good thing I have come to know and enjoy, I have received from him. Oh thank you, Jesus. I love you so.

notes

chapter 1

1. C. S. Lewis, *Mere Christianity* (New York: Macmillan, 1943, 1945, 1952), 190.

2. Lewis, *The Horse and His Boy* (New York: Macmillan, 1954), 159.

chapter 2

1. George MacDonald, *Diary of an Old Soul: 366 Writings for Devotional Reflection*, entry for June 16 (Minneapolis: Augsburg, 1965), 64.

2. Oswald Chambers, *My Utmost for His Highest: An Updated Edition in Today's Language* (Grand Rapids, MI: Discovery House, 1992).

chapter 3

1. For more on the subject, I highly recommend Lorraine Pintus, *Jump off the Hormone Swing: Fly through the Physical, Mental and Spiritual Symptoms of PMS and Perimenopause* (Chicago: Moody, 2011); and Christiane Northrup, MD, *The Wisdom of Menopause: Creating Physical and Emotional Health during the Change* (New York: Bantam, 2012).

2. Here I recommend Jean Lush and Patricia H. Rushford, *Emotional Phases of a Woman's Life* (Old Tappan, NJ: Revell, 1987).

3. Frank Sinatra, "Strangers in the Night," *Strangers in the Night* © 1966 Reprise.

4. "Ethiopian Girl Reportedly Guarded by Lions," MSNBC, June 21, 2005, www.msnbc.msn.com/id/8305836/ns/world_news-africa/t/ethiopian-girl-reportedly-guarded-lions/#.UI78qLRpfWE.

5. "Misogyny," *Merriam-Webster's Collegiate Dictionary, Eleventh Edition*, s.v. "misogyny," www.merriam-webster.com/dictionary/misogyny (accessed May 31, 2012).

6. Michael Flood, *International Encyclopedia of Men and Masculinities* (New York: Routledge, 2007), 443.

7. Sam Jolman, "Lust, Part 2: The Hangover," *www.samjolman.com*, November 20, 2011, www.samjolman.com/lust-part-2-the-hangover.

8. *Compassion Magazine*, fall 2001, 7.

9. Julie Baumgardner, "Human Trafficking," *Timesfreepress.com*, April 15, 2012, www.times-freepress.com/news/2012/apr/15/041512e2-human-trafficking/.

10. Jolman, "Lust, Part 2: The Hangover."

chapter 4

1. Mark Salzman, "Jailhouse Bach," *Reader's Digest*, May 2004.

2. Christiane Northrup, *Mother-Daughter Wisdom*, DVD (Carlsbad, CA: Hay House, 2005).

3. Phillip Moffit, "Healing Your Mother (or Father) Wound," DharmaWisdom, 2012, http://dharmawisdom.org/teachings/articles/healing-your-mother-or-father-wound.

chapter 5

1. Becky, communication with the author. Used with permission.

chapter 6

1. Dan Zadra and Kristel Wills, *5: Where Will You Be Five Years from Today?* (Seattle: Compendium, 2009), 9.

chapter 7

1. Derek Both, "Why Horror Films Are So Popular," *ABC Article Directory*, www.abcarticle-directory.com/Article/Why-Horror-Films-Are-So-Popular/91442 (accessed August 8, 2012).

2. *Dictionary.com*, s.v. "fear," dictionary.reference.com/browse/fear (accessed August 8, 2012).

chapter 8

1. John Fawcett, "Blest Be the Tie that Binds," 1782. Public domain.

2. For more on this, see Andrew Reese, *Freedom Tools: For Overcoming Life's Tough Problems*. (Grand Rapids: Chosen, 2008); and John Eldredge, *Waking the Dead* (Nashville: Nelson, 2003).

chapter 9

1. Sarah Young, *Jesus Calling* (Nashville: Integrity, 2004), 341.

chapter 10

1. *The Shawshank Redemption*, directed by Frank Darabont (Culver City, CA: Columbia Pictures, 1994).

2. Sabatina James, "Why My Mother Wants Me Dead," *Newsweek*, March 5, 2012, www.thedailybeast.com/newsweek/2012/03/04/sabatina-james-why-my-mother-wants-me-dead.html.

3. John Eldredge, *Waking the Dead* (Nashville: Thomas Nelson, 2003), 18.

4. For more here, read Eldredge, *Waking the Dead*; and Neil T. Anderson, *The Bondage Breaker* (Eugene, OR: Harvest House, 1990).

chapter 11

Epigraph. C. S. Lewis, *The Silver Chair* (New York: Macmillan, 1953), 19–21.

1. Lewis, *Silver Chair*, 21.

2. Lewis, *Silver Chair*, 21.

3. Oswald Chambers, *My Utmost for His Highest* (Uhrichsville, OH: Barbour Publishing, 1999), 120.

4. John Milton, *The Prose Works of John Milton* (London: George Bell and Sons, 1888), 329.

5. Thomas Wolfe, "God's Lonely Man," *The Hills Beyond* (Baton Rouge: Louisiana State University Press, 1935, 1936, 1937, 1939, 1941, 1969, 2000), 186.

chapter 12

1. Philip Yancey, *Where Is God When It Hurts?* (Grand Rapids, MI: Zondervan, 1990), 161.

chapter 13

1. Chaya Babu, "285 Indian Girls Shed 'Unwanted' Names," *Associated Press*, October 22, 2011, http://news.yahoo.com/285-indian-girls-shed-unwanted-names-122551876.html.

AVAILABLE
WHEREVER
BOOKS *and* EBOOKS
ARE SOLD

NEW YORK TIMES BESTSELLER

UNVEILING THE MYSTERY OF A
WOMAN'S SOUL

Captivating

REVISED *and* EXPANDED

JOHN & STASI ELDREDGE
BEST-SELLING AUTHOR OF *WILD AT HEART*

Every woman was once a little girl.
And every little girl holds in her heart
her most precious dreams.
She longs to be swept up into
a romance, to play an irreplaceable
role in a great adventure, to be
the beauty of the story. Those desires
are far more than child's play.
They are the secret to the feminine heart.

YOUR HEART MATTERS
MORE THAN ANYTHING ELSE
IN ALL CREATION.

Stasi's Free Gift for You!

RANSOMED HEART
FEATURING
STASI ELDREDGE

CORE DESIRES of
a WOMAN'S HEART

AUDIO

In a message filled with hope, healing, and humor, Stasi Eldredge shares the three core desires within every woman's heart ... and how those desires reveal the secret of who we are truly meant to be.

To receive your free audio download, simply go to RansomedHeart.com, click to the Store page, and input this title.
At checkout, type the code HEART, and you will receive this 57-minute audio download at no charge.

RANSOMED HEART

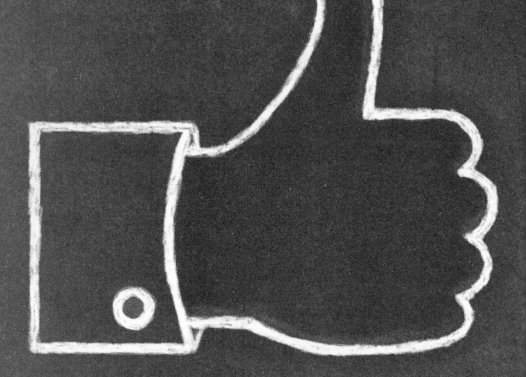

Like Stasi

f join her on facebook!